Praise for
Living into Hope: A Call to Spiritual Action for Such a Time as This

"Sermon collections are common but great sermons are rare. This is a collection of great ones. Joan Brown Campbell, in her inimitable warm, clear and penetrating way, makes scripture come alive and life more meaningful than the average day's events would ordinarily signal it to be. Read this collection of pointed and powerful sermons and begin to see both scripture and life in a new and intimate dynamic."

—**Joan Chittister, OSB**, St. Scholastica Priory; co-author,
Uncommon Gratitude: Alleluia for All That Is

"A cornucopia of relevant truths eloquently presented with sensitivity, integrity and passion.... Offers readers a rare opportunity to experience inspiration while learning history from the vivid stories of a compassionate agent. After you read this book, if you know someone who may not or cannot read this book, please read it to them."

—**Rev. Dr. C. Welton Gaddy**, president, Interfaith Alliance

"Joan Brown Campbell's prophetic words are driven by a pastor's caring heart. She lives with holy hope for all the world—and invites us also to live that way!"

—**Rev. Albert M. Pennybacker**, former pastor,
Christian Church (Disciples of Christ)

"[Unites] a remarkable life of engagement with the important and often difficult issues of our time.... A fascinating, inspiring and helpful book."

—**Rev. John M. Buchanan**, pastor, Fourth Presbyterian Church,
Chicago; editor/publisher, the *Christian Century*

"Joan Campbell's voice is an essential voice in the interfaith community today. [Here] she beautifully describes her own life experiences and how they point to the need for greater unity among the religions and understanding of our deep interdependence.... This book is a must read for all Christians and people of faith everywhere."
—**Dena Merriam**, founder and convener,
Global Peace Initiative of Women

"Joan Brown Campbell is a titan among ministers. She brings a deep love of the gospel and commitment to justice that is reminiscent of the prophetic words of Amos and the just actions of Sojourner Truth. Every person of faith will do well to read this prophetic work."
—**Rev. Otis Moss III**, senior pastor,
Trinity United Church of Christ

"Joan Campbell's vision of a world where people of every faith are honored is clearly and profoundly set forth. You will read every word again and again. As Muslim leaders, we are grateful to Joan for sharing her gifts."
—**Daisy Khan** and **Imam Feisal Abdul Rauf**,
American Society for Muslim Advancement

"These stories of faith and love are treasures that touch moments in history and share lessons for all time. Enjoy the thought-provoking discussions that emerge as you read and share my mother's life."
—**Jane Louise Campbell**, former mayor of Cleveland;
Joan Brown Campbell's daughter

"Emblematic of her inclusive theology. 'We are the Children of God,' she regularly intones, and with reverence and intent develops our understanding of the blessings and obligations of that fact."
—**Thomas M. Becker**, president, Chautauqua Institution

"Powerful testimonies from a lifetime of a pioneering Christian woman. The reflections and prayers open up the lessons we can all learn from Joan's stories. I commend the stories and the storyteller to you."
—**Jim Wallis**, president, Sojourners; author,
Rediscovering Values: On Wall Street, Main Street, and Your Street

Living into
HOPE

Living into
HOPE

A Call to Spiritual Action for Such a Time as This

REV. DR. JOAN BROWN
CAMPBELL

Foreword by Karen Armstrong

Walking Together, Finding the Way ®
SKYLIGHT PATHS®
PUBLISHING
Woodstock, Vermont

Living into Hope:
A Call to Spiritual Action for Such a Time as This

2010 Hardcover Edition, First Printing

© 2010 by Joan Brown Campbell

Foreword © 2010 by Karen Armstrong

Library of Congress Cataloging-in-Publication Data

Campbell, Joan B.
  Living into hope : a call to spiritual action for such a time as this / Joan Brown Campbell ; foreword by Karen Armstrong.
      p. cm.
  Includes bibliographical references.
  ISBN 978-1-59473-283-6 (hardcover)
  1. Hope—Religious aspects—Christianity. 2. Christian life. I. Title.
  BV4638.C235 2010
  234'.25—dc22
                                                                    2010026694

10 9 8 7 6 5 4 3 2 1

Manufactured in the United States of America
Jacket Design: Jenny Buono
Jacket Art: "Sanctus," copyright © Mélissa Bradette, from Fotolia.com
Interior Design: Kristi Menter

SkyLight Paths Publishing is creating a place where people of different spiritual traditions come together for challenge and inspiration, a place where we can help each other understand the mystery that lies at the heart of our existence.

SkyLight Paths sees both believers and seekers as a community that increasingly transcends traditional boundaries of religion and denomination—people wanting to learn from each other, walking together, finding the way.

SkyLight Paths, "Walking Together, Finding the Way," and colophon are trademarks of LongHill Partners, Inc., registered in the U.S. Patent and Trademark Office.

Walking Together, Finding the Way®
Published by SkyLight Paths Publishing
A Division of Longhill Partners, Inc.
Sunset Farm Offices, Route 4, P.O. Box 237
Woodstock, VT 05091
Tel: (802) 457-4000   Fax: (802) 457-4004
www.skylightpaths.com

This book is dedicated to my eight grandchildren. In their lives and in the lives of young people everywhere resides our hope for the future:

Alexander Campbell
Erin Campbell
Jessica Campbell-Morrison
Julie Campbell
Katie Campbell-Morrison
Lucy Campbell
Ryan Campbell
Sarah Campbell

Contents

Foreword by Karen Armstrong   xi

Acknowledgments   xv

Introduction   xvii

PART ONE: Love and Unity   1

Love Matters   3

Bearing Down in Love   11

Who Is My Neighbor?   19

One Shepherd, One Flock   27

PART TWO: Reconciliation and Renewal   35

Sacred Conversation   37

Prodigals and the Path to Peace   49

For Such a Time as This   59

The Beloved Community   67

PART THREE: Faith in Action   77

The Road to Jerusalem   79

Dangerous Dreams   89

Science and Religion   97

On Prayer   109

Discussion Guide

Introduction to the Discussion Guide   119

Love Matters   120

Bearing Down in Love   125

Who Is My Neighbor?   129

One Shepherd, One Flock   134

Sacred Conversation   138

Prodigals and the Path to Peace   142

For Such a Time as This   147

The Beloved Community   152

The Road to Jerusalem   157

Dangerous Dreams   162

Science and Religion   167

On Prayer   172

About the Discussion Guide Authors   176

Notes   177

Foreword

Karen Armstrong

Each of the great religious traditions represents a constant dialogue between a transcendent reality that is beyond time and change and the history of our world. The three Abrahamic religions have taken this very seriously, discerning a divine presence in both past and current events. Christians believe that in some profound sense, God entered human history in the person of the man Jesus. In today's terms, the prophets of Israel can be seen as political commentators; they analyzed turbulent conditions of the ancient Middle East and discerned the hand of God. The earliest biographies of the Prophet Muhammad depict him listening very carefully to the underlying meaning of the crises of the early Muslim community, sometimes sweating with the effort of bringing a divine message to his people.

In this sense, Joan Brown Campbell's career can be regarded as prophetic. She too has found a transcendent imperative in the challenges of her time. Joan always says that the pivotal moment of her life occurred when as a young woman she invited the Reverend Dr. Martin Luther King, Jr., to speak at her church in Cleveland, believing—incorrectly, as it turned out—that her community would be delighted to welcome him. Nevertheless, she pressed on, devoting herself to the civil rights movement at great personal cost, because she could see that the treatment of the African American citizens in the United States was incompatible with religion and morality, and an affront to humanity itself. In this political involvement, she found her religious vocation.

For years, as a young mother, Joan worked in the ghettoes of Cleveland; this humane and political engagement led her to the ministry. Later, she became the first woman to hold the position of general secretary of the National Council of Churches, and this great responsibility gave her the opportunity to embrace the needs of the global community. Her work with the churches of Cuba led to a lifelong determination to improve its relationship with the United States: she was, for example, instrumental in returning the Cuban boy Elián González to his father.

Joan's career reminds me of a Buddhist meditation known as "The Immeasurables," in which you extend your sympathies to the four corners of the earth, not omitting a single creature from this radius of concern. Steeped through and through with the Christian message, Joan has also learned to respect and appreciate the other great world traditions. After leaving the National Council, she became director of the religion department at the Chautauqua Institution and devoted herself wholeheartedly to its Abrahamic initiative.

In the late nineteenth century, a time of great sectarian antagonism in the northern United States, Chautauqua was founded as a place where Protestants of all persuasions could meet together in peace and mutual respect. But a century later, it was clear that this Protestant pluralism was no longer enough. It was now time to realize and rejoice in the fact that Jews, Christians, and Muslims belonged to a common family of faith.

After the atrocities of September 11, 2001, Joan, horrified by the anti-Muslim hostility sweeping the United States, called me to ask if I would become the theologian-in-residence at Chautauqua in the summer of 2002, running a program entitled "Understanding Islam." It was not an easy summer, but the difficulties we encountered forged our friendship. Most Chautauquans were anxious to learn more about Muslim practice and spirituality, but a small minority had no intention whatsoever of understanding Islam and tried to wreck the program. Joan was indomitable. She was unfailingly kind and supportive to me and warm and welcoming to the Muslim guests who came to lecture each week, but resolute in the face of the sometimes vitriolic opposition.

Like any true prophet, Joan is unflinching in the face of injustice, cruelty, unkindness, prejudice, and spite. Yet she is always fair, listening carefully and courteously to what her opponents have to say. During that hard season I chiefly became aware of the warmth of her humanity. I witnessed her intense love of her family, her affectionate devotion to friends, and her sheer enjoyment of life. However stressful things were, Joan never lost her sense of humor. Living cheek by jowl in the somewhat cramped conditions of Chautauqua's Hall of Missions for nine weeks would test anybody's friendship, but we always seemed to be laughing. In spite of everything, we had a lot of fun.

For Joan, faith has meant engagement with the world and its pain. Her spirituality has been formed not by silent meditation, but in action. By constantly going out to meet suffering and injustice wherever she finds it, Joan has developed her own form of "The Immeasurables," the Buddhist principles of loving-kindness, compassion, joy, and equanimity which, when practiced, radiate outward and touch an immeasurable number of people and do an immeasurable amount of good. Joan's "immeasurable" is based on action and practice. Constantly extending the radius of her concern in ever-wider circles, no matter what the cost, she has broken down the barriers of fear, envy, hatred, selfishness, and suspicion that keep us from our best selves and from the Divine. In the process she has become a full and enlightened human being.

It is this humanity that you will encounter in these pages. Joan is living proof that the test of true spirituality is not rigid observance but practically expressed compassion. It is no surprise to me that she has become a major figure in the creation and promotion of the Charter for Compassion, a global initiative to restore compassion and empathy to the heart of religion and morality (www.charterforcompassion.org). Joan is passionate about compassion because she has lived it.

This book will be a precious gift to those who have not had the privilege of knowing and working with Joan. It reminds us that at its best, religion should not narrow our horizons, but enable us to live more fully; should not limit our humanity, but make us wholly human; and should not cause us to withdraw from the world, but to do our utmost to make it a better place.

Acknowledgments

One cannot experience life in isolation. We are the sum total of all who have given us love and challenges and encouragement. I name here just a few people who have made life rich and full for me and whose voices are heard in the stories told in this book: my mother, Jane; my father, Dr. Jimmy; my pastor, Albert M. Pennybacker; and the Reverend Dr. Martin Luther King, Jr., whose life gave my life purpose.

I also want to thank my children, who allowed me to grow up along with them. They remain my closest friends and my most honest truth tellers: Jane Louise Campbell; Paul Barton Campbell, Jr.; and James Wiley Campbell.

A special word of grateful thanks to my sisters in the faith: Sister Joan Chittister, Karen Armstrong, Maureen Rovegno, and Barbara George.

I am also grateful to the National Council of Churches, the World Council of Churches, and the Chautauqua Institution. Each of these institutions and all those in their leadership have blessed my life. It was through these institutions that I met the world. A special note of appreciation to Tom Becker, the president of the Chautauqua Institution, who encouraged me to write this book and lovingly gave me the time to write. I also thank my assistant, Nancy Roberts, who daily keeps me on schedule and on track.

Closer to this project, my thanks go out to my editor, Nancy Fitzgerald, who has captured my voice and understood my words as they attempted to tell the stories that illustrate the themes in this book, and to SkyLight Paths for working to make this book a reality. I thank Joyce Brasted, who has transcribed my sermons, speeches, and prayers for years and catalogued and collated them for use in this book and in my other work. She worked tirelessly to collect and craft the materials and worked with the publisher to see this book to completion.

Most of all, I thank God, who has given me the courage to strive to make the decisions that have led to the life I live—courage to live into hope that this world will be a better place when I leave it than when I entered it. May this be so for all who read this book. God's blessings on you all.

Joan Brown Campbell
Chautauqua, New York

Introduction

Life can only be understood backwards;
but it must be lived forwards.
—SØREN KIERKEGAARD

I invite you to join me on a journey that began eight decades ago and continues to be filled with unexpected challenges, enriching opportunities, and fascinating encounters. The stories, reflections, and prayers you will read in the pages that follow are brief glimpses into a rich and full life that is far from finished.

I grew up in Youngstown, Ohio, in a home that was filled with love. Only as I look backward do I fully understand the power of that love and the way it cushioned me in what can only be described as an interrupted life, filled with welcome and unwelcome surprises. My father was a doctor who gave his life so that others might live. My mother gave herself to her community. It was at the feet of my parents that I learned to be a responsive and caring member of my community and, finally, of the world. But the way that learning was to play out would have amazed my parents. There have been times when it has amazed me.

It never occurred to me as a young woman that I might one day become an ordained minister. It was an unthinkable thought for a young woman growing up in the 1940s. I did what was expected of me. I graduated with honors from the University of Michigan on the day my oldest child, Jane, now herself the mother of two daughters, Jessica and Katie, was born. Jane became the first female mayor of Cleveland, Ohio, and today is chief of staff to Senator Mary Landrieu of Louisiana. Her brother Paul lives in New York City, serves as key staff to the International Baccalaureate, and is father to Sarah, a beautiful child born across the globe in China, who has enriched our lives with her love and her confident personality. And Jim, who brought up the rear, is named for his grandfather—my dad—who died at fifty-eight of a heart attack, when Jimmy was a two-year-old. Dr. Jim, my father, was present at my Jim's birth. Maybe that's why Jim, now the father of Alexander, Julie, Erin, Ryan, and Lucy, is today a highly respected and much-loved doctor at Cleveland's Metro Hospital, an institution that serves the city's poor. My eight grandchildren call me to a life of hope and continued advocacy for those whose lives are burdened with poverty and prejudice and uncertainty. They point me to a future that will be theirs to mold.

These are the bare bones of my life, and as I read them over I realize that my life sounds neat and traditional. But behind this meager biographical data lie experiences quite different from those my parents envisioned for me—or those I envisioned for myself.

My story veered off its expected course when I was thirty-two, and a minister entered my life who challenged my unexplored commitment to a life of faith. I was raised in a Christian home: my grandfather, a Presbyterian pastor, taught me the Bible and stressed the commitment necessary for every Christian. My commitment was strong, but its content was confused. When I heard the Reverend Dr. Albert Pennybacker's ecumenical and interfaith message, all the lights went on and a million unconnected pieces fell into place. I understood that faith—real, living faith—weaves together all the parts of our lives, and changes everything.

With dizzying speed, my neatly comfortable, predictable life changed. Seeing the connections between the gospel and justice, I became engaged in the civil rights movement. I met Martin Luther King, Jr.; I worked for the election of Carl B. Stokes, the first African American mayor of a major American city; I taught in Cleveland's poorest neighborhoods and encountered the depths of fear and hatred rooted in prejudice. My new life outpaced my old one, and after a while, the old one had to be discarded. My husband—a prominent attorney—had also expected a quieter, more predictable life, and a wife who would be a gracious hostess, belong to the garden club, and serve on the right committees. But I had become somebody very different, and our marriage of twenty-five years ended. The children had grown up—and I had grown up with them.

I embarked on a lengthy course of self-study, as do many who study for the ministry in the Baptist Church, and at the age of fifty I was ordained. But once again I didn't take the predictable path into parish life. My experience in the civil rights movement had transformed my faith into something broader, and called me to ecumenical and interfaith work. That work has taken me all over the country, all over the world, and has woven together my faith, my life, and my hope for the power of religion for good in society.

The chapters that follow are woven from a tapestry of hope and disappointment, of opportunity and unexpected encounters with remarkable people. Though I draw primarily from the Christian tradition, I hope people of all faiths will find inspiration in these stories and experiences. I hope that as you read this book you will not forget the uncertainties that are part of every life. I hope you will see in your own life—no matter your faith tradition—that we are all just ordinary people, but we are God's people called and created to live extraordinary lives.

My faith has carried me through illnesses, divorce, and deaths that have taken lifelong anchors of love and support from me. But my faith has also called me to engage fully in the world. There my privileged encounters with God's remarkable servants have changed me and set me on a path from which there is no way but forward.

Life has taught me that hope is born in the eye of the storm. Hope is not happiness. Rather it is the fulfillment that comes from a life that takes risks and loves deeply and falls and soars and falls and rises again. The chapters that follow are my tribute to hope.

Hope, after all, is central to Christian life. But hope is not a sweet and sappy optimism. Consider, for example, the Gospel of Mark, which ends abruptly at the empty tomb of Jesus. Mary Magdalene, Mary the mother of James, and Salome have come to anoint the body of Jesus, but they have found only a man in a white robe telling them that Jesus has gone back to Galilee. "So they went out and fled from the tomb," the gospel recounts, "for terror and amazement had seized them; and they said nothing to anyone, for they were afraid" (Mark 16:8).

That ending leaves us hanging. But we all know what happened after that—and knowing offers inspiration and hope to us two thousand years later. Those women prevailed over their fear and trembling and headed out to Galilee. They were the first to tell the story of Jesus's resurrection and they continued to encounter Jesus in their lives and their work. This ending "would be very bad news," notes biblical scholar Elaine Pagels, "if it weren't that underneath this rather dark story is an enormous hope that this very unpromising story and its terrible anguished ending is nevertheless not the ending, that there's a mystery in it, a divine mystery of God's revelation that will happen yet."[1]

This is the hope that has enriched my life at the most unexpected times and even in the most dismal circumstances. I invite you to look into your own life and see how hope has transformed you as well.

Part One

Love and Unity

God is love, and those who abide in love
abide in God, and God abides in them.
—1 JOHN 4:16

In the ministry of Jesus and his earliest followers, probably nothing was more important than love and unity—human beings were to be united with God and with one another in a love that manifested itself through prayer, community life, and selfless giving to anyone who happened to be in need.

Jesus, of course, was a model of this love and unity, which was to be extended to all people everywhere. His followers—then and now—have stumbled again and again in getting it right, but throughout the centuries, Christians have striven to embody these ideals in their lives. Every now and then, I have had a glimpse of love and unity in action.

Love Matters

*Above all, clothe yourselves with love, which binds
everything together in perfect harmony. And let the
peace of Christ rule in your hearts, to which indeed
you were called in the one body. And be thankful.*
— COLOSSIANS 3:14–15

L oss shows us what matters. This is a story of many losses, and
even more love. It starts with a small town and a small boy.

The small town is Cárdenas, one of the oldest communities in
Cuba, located near the famous beaches of Veradera. It is a place
where proud Cubans live, where many buses are still drawn by horses
to get from place to place—not like Central Park, where the carriages
clatter by for the entertainment of the tourists. It is a town where
medical clinics abound and schools command the people's serious
attention, where many are employed in the growing tourist industry,
working by day in first-class hotels and going home at night to the
modest houses where they raise their families. This property—
almost all of it—was once owned by the DuPonts, a wealthy
American industrial family, and was referred to as the DuPont Estate.
Today it is Cuban.

Water is life and livelihood in this place, but it can also be death-
dealing. Think back to the headlines that dominated the news for
months and months in 1999 and 2000. It was from this beach, from
this town, that a small boy named Elián González and his mother

boarded a small, homemade, ill-conceived vessel meant to carry six people but packed with fourteen.

This was just one of the thousands of boats—some more seaworthy than others—that have secretly set out for Florida since the Cuban Revolution and the advent of Communism in the 1960s, as Cubans sought better economic and political conditions than they found at home. Their immigration is illegal—any Cuban found at sea, heading for U.S. shores, is deported by the U.S. Coast Guard or—if discovered by Cuban police—ostracized at home. But despite the consequences, hundreds of thousands of Cubans have come to the United States, often risking their lives.[1]

News accounts reported that Elián's mother was taking him to freedom, but the story is a little more complicated. Elián's mother had left the island with her boyfriend, an ex-prisoner who made his living by taking people from Cuba to the U.S. mainland. He was paid a thousand dollars for each person he carried in that little boat—which is why it carried eight more people than it should have.

Fourteen people.

One thousand dollars apiece.

The mother's story was also complicated. Later, when I asked the Cuban officials, "Why don't you tell this part of the story?" their answer was poignant and memorable. They wanted Elián to have a good memory of a loving mother, they explained. They didn't want to harm her reputation. They wanted Elián to grow up with respect for this woman who, without question, had loved him dearly. But the fact remains that she and her boyfriend left one night in an unsafe craft and headed off across the water with this little boy, without telling his father or his grandparents.

The little aluminum boat set sail on November 21, 1999, for the ninety-mile journey from Veradera to Florida. In the best of circumstances, it would have been a fairly easy one-day trip. But the circumstances went from bad to worse. The vessel's faulty engine gave out, and fourteen-foot waves overturned the boat. Elián's mother and most of the other passengers drowned. Among the three survivors was Elián, who was found floating in an inner tube by two fishermen who thought at first that he was dead. He had been snugly and lovingly wrapped—two pairs of socks, long pants, a hat on his head and socks on his hands, prepared by his mother for survival.

When the fishermen found him, dolphins surrounding his tiny raft, they turned him over to the Coast Guard, who took him ashore to a hospital. He woke up surrounded completely by strangers and asked someone to call his father, Juan Miguel González, in Cuba. His father called Elián's grandfather's brother, who took Elián to his home in Miami—and there the struggle began. Should the child remain in the United States, where his extended family promised him a life of opportunity? Or should he be returned to his father and his family in Cuba?

Elián entered my life unexpectedly soon after he arrived in Florida, and reordered my priorities from that day to this. As general secretary of the National Council of Churches, I was asked to intervene for our government to help return Elián to his father. My involvement began as a professional endeavor, but quickly became personal.

As Elián's tragic story unfolded across the Christmas season, it brought to mind another small child at the center of hope and promise and controversy. So threatening was that small child that his parents had to spirit him away to safety. And when he grew up, he was known to welcome children among his circle of friends: we can learn, he insisted, deep and profound things from these little ones, to whom the kingdom of heaven belongs.

As I was privileged to be involved in the struggle of the González family, I often thought about the powerful lesson Elián González had to teach us. It was simple, clear, profound, and ancient. His lesson, much like the lesson of Jesus, was this: *love matters.*

Elián needed to go home to those who loved him, to those who were ready and able to care for him. Back in Cárdenas, his father, his father's new wife, and their four-month-old baby, along with Elián's maternal and paternal grandparents and his great-grandmother, awaited. It was these loving, caring people who watched and waited as our political system, our courts, and our agencies determined the future of their loved one—this very small boy.

While the various bureaucracies were reviewing the "case" and trying to decide what to do, I spent two days with Elián's family. We met in their home in the little town of Cárdenas, with no government officials present. I saw firsthand the strength of this family and their bonds of love and affection. Their grief was palpable. Their desire to have Elián home came from deep within their hearts.

But the family in Miami did not seem to understand. When reporters asked him why they believed that Elián should stay in the United States, the uncle responded that Elián's father had nothing to give this child but love.

I had to listen twice to believe what I had heard.

My daughter, Jane, at that time a commissioner in Cuyahoga County, Ohio, called me in astonishment when she heard that statement. On that very day in her county, she said, there were over five thousand children in protective custody because they had no one to love them.

Love is the most powerful force in the world. It is the one thing that children cannot be without. To grow up to be a stable, productive adult, every book, every parenting guide, every psychiatrist will tell you that parental love is the key.

When I came back from Cuba, I was asked one question over and over by the media: "Reverend Campbell, can you, beyond the shadow of a doubt, guarantee that there has been no coercion of the González family by the Cuban government?"

It was an irrelevant question. I had watched the loving gestures as Elián's family dried one another's tears of sadness and grief. I had seen on their faces only their heartfelt fear that Elián might never return. I had observed the powerlessness they felt, not at the hands of the Cuban government but at the hands of the United States' courts. I had felt their pride as they showed us their modest home, Elián's room, his simple toys—an enormous contrast to the shiny new bikes and the trips to Disney World that tempted him in Miami.

Down in Cárdenas, there was only a modest house in a simple village, and a family's loss and love that were powerful, compelling, raw. Elián's maternal grandmother, speaking with me, said, "I don't talk much, and I'm very frightened of the cameras, but I want to tell you that I have lost my only daughter. All I have left is this little boy, Elián, my grandson. And it is my desire that Juan Miguel raise that child in this house with his new wife and baby." That family's struggle, their loss, and their deep love of this one little child bring us back again to what really matters in this life. A little boy spent two days alone at sea, adrift on an inner tube, and suddenly was offered all the "good things" America had to offer. When people asked him, "Do you want to stay here?" did we really expect him to be lured by the toys that had come his way? His mother was gone, his home was across the sea, and he just wanted to be with his father. He talked with his father whenever he was allowed to do so.

What became clear to me during my visit with Elián's family was that the only right choice was to do whatever must be done to reunite this family. As people of faith, our call, first of all, is to love— an active, passionate love that softens and molds and strengthens who we are. Paul writes in his first letter to the Corinthians, "Now faith, hope, and love abide, these three; and the greatest of these is love" (1 Corinthians 13:13).

Getting to know Elián and his family reminded me of the importance of love and unity. The bonds of love needed to be honored; the unity of the family from that little Cuban village needed to be respected. And people of all faiths and cultures need to unite to accomplish the work of love and unity in our world. I experienced the love of this family: the youthful vigor of the father, and the fragility of the great-grandmother. She looked at the cross I was wearing and told me that she didn't know about the rest of her family but she was a praying person, and she prayed fervently for her little grandson's safe return.

In the face of love so amazing, the story of Elián brings us to our knees. The love of father for son, son for father, is not about courts or lawyers or governments. It is about the human capacity to love. And that is central to Christian life.

I think back to the day that Juan Miguel González and I sat in a living room in Cuba with his closest friends and trusted companions. We had just told him that if he wanted his boy back, he would have to risk coming to the United States to get him. He could be pulled into a lengthy court battle, separated from his new baby and his wife.

Juan Miguel, embraced by Ricardo Alarcón, president of the Cuban parliament, looked squarely at me and asked me to promise him that if he went, he would be able to bring his boy home.

I couldn't make that promise. I told him instead, "You will have to take that risk—that leap of faith. But I can tell you this: If you do not go, you will not get your boy back." And with one arm around him and one holding Ricardo Alarcón's hand, we promised him we would walk with him all the way.

And so he went, not knowing. He went on faith, believing but not believing. Most of all, he went on love. Juan Miguel's young bride and their new baby went with him.

I will always carry in my memory the reunion of father and son aboard the U.S. plane that brought Elián home from Florida. Tears streaming down his face, Juan Miguel cradled his son and with love in his eyes, he said, "Elián, I never thought I'd see you again."

■

There is a postlude to this story that speaks to the ongoing power of love that connects us across oceans and cultures and unspeakable loss. I was sitting in a clothing store, waiting while my fourteen-year-old granddaughter tried on jeans, when my cell phone rang.

The voice on the other end said in Spanish, "Mama, mama, are you all right?"

I listened to the voice, and asked, "Elián?"

And he said, "Mama. Elián González. Elián."

Then his father got on the phone, and suddenly I was talking with Juan Miguel González, who said, "We just want to know that you are all right. We just want to know that your people are all right. Would you do something for me?"

Juan Miguel, a Cuban citizen, asked me to tell the American people how much he loved them and how sorry Cubans were for everything that had happened, for everyone who was suffering.

It was September 11, 2001.

This simple man who lives on an island in very modest circumstances was able to separate the difference between American policy on Cuba and the American people. This was a man who understood, deep down, about the profound unity that exists—no matter the politics or the theology or the color of their skin—between people who love one another.

REFLECT

The story of Elián González is a story of love and unity that tugged at the heartstrings of the world as it played out in the press over a decade ago. But love and unity are not simply sentimental ideas—they are the work of faith and courage. Reflect on an occasion in your own life when you made the decision to reach out in unity. How did your faith sustain your efforts?

PRAY

So, my friend and neighbor,
what does the Lord require of us?
To love the Lord your God with
all your heart, with all your soul,
and with all your mind,
and your neighbor as yourself.

If we do this we will live in
peace with one another.
The social fabric will be knit anew.
America's every flaw will
have been mended by the
God who created and placed
us in this world neighborhood
and who calls us to love one another.

Bearing Down in Love

I therefore, the prisoner in the Lord, beg you to lead a life worthy of the calling to which you have been called, with all humility and gentleness, with patience, bearing with one another in love.
—EPHESIANS 4:1–2

A house divided against itself cannot stand.
—MATTHEW 12:25

On the eve of the Civil War, America was locked in a struggle so deep, a conflict of values so profound, that the life—even the soul—of the nation was at stake. Abraham Lincoln, borrowing from the Gospel of Matthew, spoke one of history's oft-quoted lines when he won the nomination for the Illinois Senate seat in 1858: "I believe this government cannot endure permanently," he said, "half slave and half free."[1] From the depths of his being, Lincoln understood the need for unity.

The system of slavery tore everything asunder—political and economic structures, religious bodies, friendships, families. Many years ago, I saw a movie called *The Slaves* and I have never forgotten it. The images from one scene of a family torn apart are seared on my soul. On the steps of a city hall in South Carolina, a sign announced, "Auction today—2:00 p.m." The items to be sold, of course, were human beings—slaves. The camera focused in on a handsome young man and a pregnant woman, holding on to each other for dear life.

The auctioneer called the young man forward. "What am I bid for this handsome young buck?" he demanded. "Take a look at him; he can pull a plow, he can till the soil. Take a very good look at him. Look at that handsome face. He could serve at your table." The bidding was quick and lively and the man was sold for a very high price. As he was being led away by his new owner, his tear-filled eyes looked back at his sobbing wife and the auctioneer hammered the deal to a close. It was the end of that family. Did they ever see each other again? The movie never reveals the answer, but history tells us that the chances were very slim.

Any nation that so callously disregards family structures—that breaks the unifying bonds of love, caring, and responsibility—must, with heart and voice, confess its sinfulness and pray for forgiveness. Abraham Lincoln's dream of unity was realized: slavery was abolished and the country was reunified. But that's not the end of the story. History is lived out today, and "the sins of the fathers were visited on the next generation and the next" (Exodus 34:6–7).

Today, America's noble national dream is still at odds with reality. We are still a nation divided in many ways, even if not so overtly as by slavery. We are at times divided by class, by gender, by religion—and, sadly, still by race. Perhaps we are a nation that needs to remind ourselves again of just how crucial unity is.

Think of New York: it is a city as diverse as any metropolis in the world, and that it works at all is one of God's greatest surprises. The shining jewel of this place isn't on Wall Street or at the Empire State Building or in the Metropolitan Museum of Art. New York's riches are on every street corner, from Brooklyn to the Bronx—they are its people. They come from every place in the world—the Korean greengrocers and the Somali cab drivers and the newly arrived workers from Eastern Europe. They are God's people who struggle to survive, who fuss and fume with one another, who can sometimes be brutal to one another. They experience ethnic rivalries and racial tensions and economic injustices. But, when push comes to shove, they can reach for the high promise of God's greatest gift, the gift of our unity. On the days after 9/11, this city of eight million pulled together like a small village to help one another grieve and to put life back together again.

As Christians—as human beings—unity must be our polar star. Jesus prayed for it; Lincoln strove toward it; New Yorkers struggle with it day by day. The apostle Paul, ministering to his hodgepodge collection of communities, knew how hard unity could be. "Bear with one another in love" (Ephesians 4:2), he wrote to his bickering friends in the city of Ephesus, in what is now Turkey. For human beings to bear with other human beings, Paul knew from experience, can be difficult and painful.

But of course it can also be fruitful. Consider, for example, an alternative meaning of the verb *to bear*. For anyone who has ever birthed a child or stood at the side of a woman giving birth, the words *bear down* take on special meaning. When the pain seems unbearable, when the mother believes she cannot go on, just then—in the midst of the chaos—someone tells her to "bear down." New life breaks through the agony and the suffering blurs into memory, washed away by the joy of life itself.

Today, the noble dream of unity—and the imperfect reality—still seem to be at odds, in America and around the world. We are still divided and torn asunder in many, many ways. Perhaps more than ever we need to turn to the image of family to help us internalize anew the faithful response of unity.

Family, of course, is an important image for all people of faith. Jesus called those who followed him his family: "Whoever does the will of my Father in heaven is my brother and sister and mother" (Matthew 12:50). Paul the apostle called the members of his new Christian communities his "beloved children" (1 Corinthians 4:14). And today, two thousand years later, Christians still gather regularly as family at a common table of love and grace and mercy and forgiveness. Yet some speak of "family values" as if they were describing an exclusive club, for members only. This narrow view is not the one that leads to unity. Our family of faith needs to reach out and embrace everyone.

Too many of us feel responsible only for our own kith and kin. According to a 2007 Census Bureau report, 37.3 million Americans live in poverty;[2] around the world people die daily of preventable diseases and in the developing world too many mothers die in childbirth. These things worry and perplex us and engage us in conversation, both private and public. But do we define them as *family* matters? Do we sit around our kitchen table and say, "This is a family concern"? As people of faith, caring for our own households and relatives is not our *only* job. We need to draw the lines of family in a way that is large, generous, and inclusive.

The Christian view of family is about unity and oneness. It is about our interdependence and our deep interrelationship. Our family includes our children and grandchildren and cousins, as well as our next-door neighbors and people of different religions and ethnicities—indeed, our entire global family.

As people of faith, we are called to broaden the family circle, to grant family status to the stranger. In the words of Rabbi Joachim Prinz, a renowned Jewish leader and civil rights advocate, in an address to the 1963 March on Washington, "Neighbor is not a geographical term. It is a moral concept."

And Jesus, of course, in the parable of the good Samaritan, instructed us to number even our enemies among those we care about—and for. Family values for all people of faith must include a large and very diverse gathering of people: people whose names we will never know, people whose faces we will never see, people we do not agree with or do not even like much.

We need to be called back to this expansive, biblical notion of family and unity. We need to take hold of this issue of family values. We need to see, with the eyes of faith, the dangers that lurk when we restrict and exclude. We need to understand the consequences of exclusivity.

My son-in-law, Hunter Morrison, defines a family as a group of people with a special responsibility for one another. He also says there is often at least one person in the family in crisis at all times. Now this tells you a little bit about his family and mine, but implicit in that light-hearted definition is the maxim that the whole family is expected to bring their energy, wisdom, love, and caring to that person who is in crisis. (And if the family is lucky, there'll be just one crisis at a time.)

Think for a few moments what that attitude would mean for people caught in disasters—for the victims of earthquakes in Haiti and Chile, for the children in Iraq and Afghanistan, for the families of Zimbabwe and Darfur, for the poor in Detroit, Delhi, Dallas, Manchester. Think how seeing them as family might inform our national debates about health care, immigration, and jobs. In a healthy family, everyone sits at the same table and shares the same food. If there is a scarcity, the babies, the old folks, the pregnant mothers—and if there is a stranger, a guest—they all get the first and the biggest share.

In his letter to the Ephesians, Paul helps us understand the nature of our global family, and what it would take to create unity within this unwieldy and sometimes dysfunctional group. Listen to Paul's words:

> I therefore, the prisoner in the Lord, beg you to lead a life worthy of the calling to which you have been called, with all humility and gentleness, with patience, bearing with one another in love, making every effort to maintain the unity of the Spirit in the bond of peace.
> —EPHESIANS 4:1–3

At a National Council of Churches board meeting, I once listened to the Reverend Dr. Jim Andrews, former stated clerk of the Presbyterian

Church (USA), as he said, "If Jesus were not so insistent on unity, we wouldn't bother with it. It's entirely too much trouble." But no matter how unsettling it may be, the Bible makes it clear that we are related to one another—and not casually. You and I, and all people everywhere, are related by the call to "bear with one another in love." This is our call to family unity. We are called to walk through the pain, through the unbearable moments, bearing with one another, and bearing down until we are the one people God intends us to be.

Here's what that can look like. When apartheid was dismantled and a truly democratic election took place in South Africa, I was there to serve as an election official. I was there, too, when Nelson Mandela was inaugurated as the first African president of South Africa in 1994. During the event, Mandela told me, he noticed way in the back of the crowd the man who had been his jailer during the twenty-seven years he had been in prison for his anti-apartheid activism and his leadership in the African National Congress's armed wing. Mandela called this man's name and invited him to come forward and sit with his own family. In that single gesture, he redefined the meaning of neighbor and the meaning of family.

The challenge facing the entire world in this millennium is claiming, respecting, and affirming our diversity and the growing pluralism of our people while maintaining the bond of unity. As the Christian tradition tells us, it will require a commitment to unity that is in our hearts, not just our minds.

If we read the Bible carefully, we will find a strong emphasis on inclusion. When Jesus called himself the shepherd, he even said, "I have other sheep that do not belong to this fold. I must bring them also, and they will listen to my voice. So there will be one flock, one shepherd" (John 10:16). Those of us who claim the name Christian dare not see any people as nobody, for God has called everyone "God's people." In the ecumenical community, we understand that our responsibility is for all who are created in God's image, and who—*who?*—do we dare suggest be excluded?

It is our gift and our inescapable calling to be one people.

Martin Luther King, Jr., once said, "Love is the most durable power in the world. This creative force, so beautifully exemplified in the life of our Christ is the most potent instrument available in mankind's quest for peace and security."[3] Perhaps, just perhaps, if we could live in the whole world, our smaller world would seem more manageable. For as we grasp the vision of unity, invest ourselves in the lives of others, and bear down in love, we will give birth to God's dream for us.

REFLECT

It's easy—most of the time—to see the value of unity among our own families and neighbors. What is more difficult is to grasp the importance of unity among groups who seem unconnected and vastly different: undocumented immigrants, or people from the "wrong" neighborhood, or even fellow Christians who understand the gospel in a different way than we do. Think about why unity with these "others" is crucial too. What are some small ways you can work toward that unity?

PRAY

Today, God of all people, we light a candle of hope that brings light into the darkness. Holy God, we pray today that you who created us for loving and caring might move among us, that we might be infused with your love and offer that very love to all people. We live among the richness of your creation: people whose languages we do not know, people who are different from ourselves, people who call to God by many names. May we be touched by your majestic gift of life to all your children and by your love that exceeds our capacity to imagine. We pray for wisdom for the living of these days.

We pray as well today for our world: for all who live in fear, facing an uncertain future, and for those who wander as refugees. May all find a home where they may put the sharp burden down.

O Holy God, we pray for the peacemakers, that they might be valiant and tireless in their efforts. Grant to them a glimpse of your future world for your people—a future to which we are all called.

We pray for leaders everywhere, that they might be emboldened to take up the task of peace and justice. Protect the soldiers caught in the web of war, and give them the heart for peace.

And now gracious God, you who came to be in our deepest suffering and our moments of irreverent joy, we are made bold to pray for those nearest and dearest to us. For those in our community who face illness of body, we pray for healing and an end to suffering. And now in the silence we pray quietly for all those whose lives need your truth and your tender care.

Lord, hear our prayer:

> Our Father, who art in heaven, hallowed be thy name,
> thy kingdom come, thy will be done, on earth as it is in heaven.
> Give us this day our daily bread.
> And forgive us our trespasses, as we forgive those who tres-
> pass against us.
> And lead us not into temptation, but deliver us from evil.
> For thine is the kingdom, and the power, and the glory for ever
> and ever.
> Amen.

Who Is My Neighbor?

*"Which of these three, do you think, was a neighbor
to the man who fell into the hands of robbers?" The
expert in the law replied, "The one who showed him
mercy." Jesus said to him, "Go and do likewise."*
—LUKE 10:36–37

Flip a coin—any coin. Every time we fish in our pockets for money
at a toll booth, or dig into our change purse to buy a newspaper,
we will find—if we look closely enough—a message from God:
E pluribus unum. Out of many, one.

No matter how different we are, we are all in this life together.

E pluribus unum is a treasured part of our national rhetoric. It is
emblazoned on the Great Seal of the United States and on every single
American coin. American diversity goes back to the thirteen
colonies, which had more of a racial and ethnic mix than we may
realize. Our pluralistic, patchwork-quilt society evolved not only
through successive waves of willing immigrants, but also through
the forced entry of African people who came to our shores as slaves.
Our national dream of liberty and justice for all has constantly
expanded through the years to include the rights of women, and
hopefully someday it will fully embrace the rights of gay and lesbian
people. The circle of acceptance constantly expands.

The *pluribus* part of the motto is a given; we know there are many
of us and that we come in many varieties. It's the *unum* part that has

always been problematic. But we continue to work on it. In recent years we have cast aside the "melting pot" metaphor—after all, who wants a nation whose parts have been boiled to oblivion?—and turned to the notion of our country as a mosaic, where each unique, luminous, colorful tile contributes to the great big picture that honors the cultural integrity of the collective. Only in this way can each individual, each family, each community add to the whole from a position of strength and vitality.

The ideal of *E pluribus unum* has been tough from the get-go, and not just in America. The first-century Mediterranean world that is depicted in the stories of Jesus and the writings of the early church in the Christian scriptures was also a landscape far more pluralistic than we may realize. There were Jews and Greeks and Macedonians and Asians; there were believers and practitioners of a dizzying array of religions; there were countless cultural traditions and languages and histories; and there were deep and long-standing political rivalries. So when a young lawyer asked Jesus, "Who is my neighbor?" (Luke 10:29), it was not a rhetorical question. It was a pretty tough question to answer.

Jesus answers, as he so often does, by telling a story. This one is about a traveler on a lonely road who is beaten, robbed, and left for dead, then nursed and cared for not by his own people but by a Samaritan—a member of a group that the young lawyer and most of Jesus's listeners despised. The Samaritans and the Jews, after all, had been bitter rivals for more than five hundred years. But Jesus tells this young man that the Samaritan—the one he has been taught to hate—is his neighbor. And through this story, Jesus is telling each of us that the stranger, the unaccepted one, is the person we are supposed to love and care for.

Maybe the young man's question was really this: can we limit the number of people for whom we are expected to care? I think Jesus would answer today as he did back then: we are to show mercy, to be neighborly, to all, regardless of national origin, religion, race, or anything else. As the great theologian John Wesley, the founder of Methodism, so wisely said, "I look upon all the world as my parish;... in whatever part of it I am, I judge it meet, right, and my bounden duty to declare unto all that are willing to hear the glad tidings of salvation. This is the work which I know God has called me to, and sure I am that his blessing attends it."[1]

We are all neighbors, Jesus insists. We are all in this together. Unity matters—and it matters more as the world grows closer and as our neighborhood becomes larger and larger. Our challenge today is to come to grips with the interdependence of the world community. For Americans who celebrate our independence, the motto of the founding fathers still serves. But the "many" who must become "one" speak different languages, come from different cultures, worship God in many different ways, and are separated by oceans and mountains, rivers and streams—yet are united by a communication system that gives us the play-by-play of war as it happens. We are united to mothers and children in Iraq and Afghanistan, to factory workers in China, to the people who staff the computer help desks in the call centers in India. And oddly enough, we are even united to life forms on Mars, as I learned from my friend and mentor Carl Sagan, the astrophysicist, author, and producer of the hugely popular 1980 television series *Cosmos.*

Every time we got together, Carl, a self-proclaimed agnostic, would say to me, "You're so smart, Joan—why do you believe in God?" And I would look him straight in the eye and demand, "And *you're* so smart, Carl—why *don't* you believe in God?" Though he was not a believer, he had an expansive view of what it means to be a neighbor. In ways that amazed us, religion and science had lessons to teach us both.

Carl was passionately curious about interterrestrial life, and explored its possibility with the care and precision of his craft. Toward the end of his life, a meeting took place in the White House, inspired by Carl and called together by then Vice President Al Gore, with thirty interdisciplinary Nobel laureates in science, to discuss the likelihood of life on Mars.

This is not my area of expertise, and nobody was more surprised than I was to have been invited to this event. PBS religion journalist Bill Moyers and I were the only two representatives of the world of religion, and we felt very much like fish out of water.

As the meeting proceeded, Bill Moyers wrote me a note: "What are we doing here?" The dazzling discussion was way over our heads, so I followed my own advice and did what I always tell students to do: when you feel like that, be very, very quiet. I listened intently, breathless with excitement, and as soon as the meeting was over I grabbed a notebook and scribbled everything I could remember about what was said.

I will never forget the moment when the scientists looked at one another and declared, "We know there is microbial life on Mars. We *know* it." All the conditions for life are present there, they said, but they still could not prove it absolutely and did not want to go there to prove it until they were prepared to go as a team, not as individual missions tromping around Mars and destroying the evidence. "It is," they insisted, "just a matter of time until we can prove it to be true."

It was not the presence of the vice president, or the setting in the White House, or the impending death of my friend Carl Sagan, or the glittering array of brilliant scientists that moved me. It was their message. Life, they said, must be defined as *all* of creation, not just human life.

Sadly, though he convened the meeting, Carl Sagan was unable to attend. He was in the hospital at that time, battling the cancer that would soon claim his life. The letter he wrote to the group gathered in the White House was dictated to his wife, Annie, with his last breath. It was a brief and holy message: "Life matters." As I heard those words, I thought, *This man is a believer without acknowledging it.*

Carl's letter spoke of the destructiveness of what he called "the human conceit." In religious language, we call it sin, but I think we are talking about the same thing—our human penchant to assume special privileges, to assume that we are at the center of it all, to assume the world is exclusively ours. After all, as the psalmist asked a few thousand years ago, "What are human beings that you are mindful of them?" (Psalm 8:4).

But it is not all about us. *All* of life, Carl and his fellow scientists insisted, is connected. In this galaxy of planets, everything relates to everything. Diversity is essential in the biosphere, and total independence is always death. *Always.* That makes interdependence not just a noble ideal but essential to the preservation of life. "For our world to continue to exist," one of the scientists declared, "we must have an ecumenical, nonhierarchical, unifying, integrated strategy." She used the word *ecumenical* in its largest sense to include all faiths, all peoples, the whole creation, our world, and all the worlds yet unknown. A very expansive neighborhood indeed—out of many, one. This brilliant array of scientists understood ecumenism as a way of thinking that brings down the barriers that divide us.

The Greek meaning of the word *ecumenical* has the same root as *ecology* and *economy*. Literally, it means "all of one household." That day, in that setting, Nobel scientists were saying that the future will be ecumenical and interdependent—or there will be no future at all. The scientists affirmed the vision of respected and necessary diversity working together in unity as the basis for life. The planet is in fact one interwoven web of life.

At this point in the meeting I looked again at Bill Moyers. This time, he passed me a note that said, *"Now I know why we're here."*

No reporters were allowed to cover this meeting, so that participants could speak freely, but at the end, of course, they gathered with microphones and notebooks and lots of questions. My memory of this encounter is very strong and, I admit, negative. A reporter whose name I do not recall asked me if I thought the discovery of life on Mars might affect organized religion. Before I could respond, she pointed out that Martians might look like lizards, and wondered how that would affect our understanding of God.

It seemed to me that the reporter was a bit confused. God is not made in our image—*we* are made in *God's* image. I have seen Chinese people paint God as Chinese, Africans paint God as African, women paint God as female. So why not Martians who would paint God as a lizard? God is so large, so inclusive—yet we constantly try to put God into a box and reduce God to somebody who looks just like us.

I believe in a God who is large enough to have created worlds unknown to us. I believe in a God whose way is to integrate, to heal, and to make whole. I believe in a God of unity. And if we made this simple theological point clear and lived it out, racism, sexism, and homophobia would be things of the past. Good religion encourages a way of life steeped in renewal, redemption, and rebirth, which, in turn provide the freedom to care, to risk, to step out into the unknown, acknowledging a stranger or an enemy as a neighbor.

Religion at its best leads to a sense of trust and wondrous gratitude for the human capacity to share joy, to know love, to live in relationship, to be neighbors, to be one. In such dislodging of the human conceit, the human capacity is truly freed. We are not separated from one another, but inexorably bound together. Everyone relates to everyone. Everything relates to everything. This is the only possible strategy for combating the sin of exclusion, the mistaken notion of privilege, the destructive hoarding of power. The possibility of other worlds should be of less concern to us than the divisions in this world that mute our voices and weaken our witness. Here in this world, humans fragment; God unites. Humans specialize; God makes whole.

Ecumenism at its core is a way of seeing reality. It is a radical way of being. It is a life-changing methodology for doing. If loving my neighbor is a moral mandate, then my time is not mine alone. My money is not mine to hoard. My talents are to be shared. I am to share in full and generous measure what was shared with me. It is a radical understanding of life. My world cannot be small, confined, filled with people who look and think like I do.

The answer to the question, who is my neighbor? is critical to us as people of faith and as citizens. We need, as the scientists said, the rich diversity of our planet. We need each other desperately. Going it alone, as the scientists pointed out, is ultimately death-dealing. Life is found when everything relates to everything. We dare not tire of the ecumenical call to be family, nor of the international mandate to be neighbors. We dare not get bored with or cynical about this call, for it is God's gift and challenge to us. It is sound science and good—very good—religion.

After all, out of many, we are one.

REFLECT

Recall a time when your faith led you to "a sense of trust and wondrous gratitude" for creation—perhaps a night sky or the smell of newly mowed grass or the power of a thunderstorm or the birth of a baby. Consider the deep connection between faith and the natural world.

PRAY

What does the Lord your God require of you?
To love the Lord your God
With all your heart, with all your soul,
And with all your mind,
And your neighbor as yourself.

One Shepherd,
One Flock

I am the good shepherd. I know my own and my own know me, just as the Father knows me and I know the Father. And I lay down my life for the sheep. I have other sheep that do not belong to this fold. I must bring them also, and they too will listen to my voice. So there will be one flock, one shepherd.

—JOHN 10:14–16

I grew up in a loving but very strict Presbyterian family, the grand-daughter of a Bible professor at Muskingum College in New Concord, Ohio. When we were little children, Grandfather no diminutive "Gramps" for this Calvinist soldier of the faith!—expected my sister and me to memorize great swaths of scripture. Each time he came to our home he would test us to see if we had learned the passages he had assigned. Family lore maintains that when I was five years old, I could repeat from memory the first chapter of Genesis. But when I asked Grandfather *why* he required these enormous feats of memory, the answer made less sense than the grueling act of memorization. We memorized scripture, he explained, to prepare us for that day when, for our faith, we might end up in prison without a Bible. This scenario seemed highly improbable to the daughters of a middle-class doctor. But learn the Bible we did—the King James Version, of course—and those texts are engraved on my memory to this day.

My forays into jail for various protests were short-lived and allowed little time for reciting the Bible. But over the course of my ecumenical life, I have encountered those who have, in fact, been imprisoned for their firmly held beliefs and all of them—every single one—declared that they had drawn strength from the memory of Bible texts that flooded in on them and gave them peace. So perhaps Grandfather was right. The faith of my childhood was passionate and disciplined and it has, over the years, stood me in good stead. But it was a faith with limits that was biblically grounded and replete with rules. It was a very conservative faith that allowed little room for ambiguity.

To mature in the faith meant that I needed to explore for myself the complexity of biblical truths. It meant that I needed to give myself permission to question and then to believe anew. It meant that I needed to move beyond my purely Presbyterian roots to a sense of the unity of all God's children. And from there, it was just a short hop to the larger world—the embrace of the ecumenical was inevitable. My rootedness in the Bible was the very thing that allowed me to move beyond my limited, childlike faith to the profound reality that no denomination or communion or faith possesses the whole truth. Jesus's gift of life is the starting place. His truth is not denominational and—though this may be a radical thought—it may in fact be true that we are called to embrace not just our own faith but also the unfamiliar faiths of others.

One of our great illusions is that we believe that somehow we can attest to God's love amid our foolish divisions and carefully drawn denominational differences. We are fearful, after all, of losing our distinctiveness as Presbyterians or Lutherans or Methodists or Catholics. But we really don't have to worry; we are not likely to lose our identity, or our sense of who we are, if we take the risk of being one, as Jesus prayed we would be. After all, we are each unique and distinctive in God's eyes. God knows us and claims each and every one of us as his own: "I know my own and my own know me," insists

Jesus the Good Shepherd (John 10:14). But lest we become prideful, he also acknowledges others who are not part of our flock.

God never told us to divide ourselves up. Our job is simple: to know the voice and the call of our shepherd. It is the shepherd's job to define who is in the flock and who is not. "I lay down my life for the sheep," says Jesus, "I have other sheep that do not belong to this fold. I must bring them also, and they will listen to my voice. So there will be one flock, one shepherd" (John 10:15–16). At the time this gospel was written, scholars think, there was division and disunity among the groups of people who followed the teachings of Jesus. So the future prospect of unity would have been a freeing and liberating reality to people of faith in the first century, just as it is to us today.

Think of the time, energy, pain, and suffering that human beings have put into figuring out who is in and who is out. We have separated people by race, by gender, by class, by denomination, by national identity, by age, by sexual identity, and by a thousand other petty details—all of them feeble and faithless attempts to undo Jesus's command that we love one another. We have resorted to war and violence to justify our divisions and draw lines around our little flocks and separate insiders and outsiders, enemies and friends.

What we have not done very much is to listen carefully to the passage about the good shepherd. There is only one shepherd, it proclaims, so there can be only one flock—a worldwide flock that the shepherd calls us to feed, house, clothe, nurture, and love, beyond boundaries, accidents of birth, and faith systems that are unfamiliar to us. Following our shepherd is the way to justice and peace. The question for our day is not only "Can we hear the shepherd's voice?" but also "Are we prepared to respond to it? Will we abandon our divisions and put our energy and our imagination into serving God's people everywhere?"

To work for unity is no small thing. It is to involve ourselves in the lives of people whose faces we may never see, whose names we may never call. In the late 1950s and throughout the 1960s, the civil rights movement gained momentum as African Americans struggled against social and economic discrimination. Martin Luther King, Jr., became the movement's most recognized and respected leader until his assassination in 1968. He lived a life of commitment to unity through racial justice and reconciliation that flowed not just from the color of his skin, not just from his personal experience of suffering, but from his Christian heart and soul that saw the glory of God. He internalized the future of God's flock, where there were no more tears, no more senseless killing, no more divisions.

In one of Dr. King's final speeches, given at New York City's Riverside Church on April 4, 1967, he called for our loyalties to be "ecumenical rather than sectional"—it was the only way, he insisted, to serve and to save humankind. For all ecumenists, for all those who pray for unity and renewal of our broken human community, both serving and saving the broken human community are part and parcel of our calling. For it is the cries of God's people, the groaning of creation that makes the sin of our disunity incandescently clear.

If we are to bring an end to racism and poverty, then we need more than Presbyterians or Episcopalians or Disciples going it alone. If we are to be peacemakers, then Roman Catholics and Protestants, Buddhists, Jews, Hindus, and Muslims all need to find common ground. If we are to be agents of reconciliation, then we Christians must model a table fellowship that is gracious and hospitable and welcoming. Jews and Muslims also pray for unity, so that the children of Abraham might together serve the purpose of the God who is father of us all. One flock is the only way to go.

Is this just unrealistic talk? Fine for theologians and academics and church bureaucrats, but highly improbable in the real world in which most of us live?

How dare we think that if unity does not come by our prayers, our hands, then we have a right to give up! Who hopes for what they see? We hope for what we do not see, and we wait—and work—for it with patience. Every January for more than a century we have observed a week of prayer for Christian unity. It would be easy to say, "If it has not come in all this time, then what hope is there?" But is it just possible that our work joins with all that has gone before to create an unending prayer for unity? Isn't it possible that our work continues to create a climate where divisions offend us and unity attracts us? Ours is not to complete the task; it is to run with perseverance the race that is set before us, trusting that God will intercede for the saints according to his will. If we cannot trust, then there is in fact no hope. But if we can trust, then we dare to commit ourselves anew to the quest for the unity of the church and the renewal of our broken human community.

In 1998, on one of his many visits to the National Council of Churches, Cardinal Edward Idris Cassidy of the Pontifical Council for Promoting Christian Unity spoke to this very question of the hopelessness of our time. The search for Christian unity, he said, is like climbing a very steep mountain. When the climb begins, the mountaineers are cheered and lauded for their courage, their bravery, their willingness to risk their lives. But as they proceed up the mountain and out of sight, the crowd forgets them and the climbers are alone with only their vision to inspire them. They come to a point where they must either turn back or press forward. If they decide to go forward, there will come a time when they cannot go back. In order to sustain life, they must proceed. As Cassidy remarked, we are at that point, too. We are out of sight of the cheering crowd, with only the vision of the mountaintop to sustain us.

Perhaps we can turn to Dr. King for inspiration and guidance on our journey. In his very last sermon, delivered on April 3, 1968, in support of striking sanitation workers at Mason Temple in Memphis, Tennessee, he said:

> We've got some difficult days ahead. But it doesn't matter
> with me now. Because I've been to the mountaintop.... I
> just want to do God's will. And He's allowed me to go up

to the mountain. And I've looked over. And I've seen the promised land. I may not get there with you. But I want you to know tonight, that we, as a people will get to the promised land. And I'm happy tonight. I'm not worried about anything. I'm not fearing any man. Mine eyes have seen the glory of the coming of the Lord.[1]

Like those who have gone before us up the mountain, we can return to the vision of unity that Jesus articulated in the story of the good shepherd and make it our vision too. That vision can sustain us as we continue to work toward an ecumenical, interreligious dream.

As people of faith, as members of the human race, we believe in a God whose way is to integrate, to heal, and to make whole. It is the ecumenical, interfaith way. We believe in a God large enough to have created worlds unknown to us. Our faith encourages a way of life steeped in renewal, redemption, and rebirth—which in turn provides the freedom to care, to risk, to step out into the unknown. That is the kind of faith found in people who understand themselves to be related to God, the ultimate reality that religion affirms. The interfaith pilgrimage is God's gift and challenge to us, for ultimately, we all belong to the same flock and the same shepherd.

REFLECT

Can you believe passionately in your own expression of faith and yet accept and honor the faiths of others as equally passionate for them in the living of their lives? What are some examples of this interfaith dialogue from your own life, or from the lives of people you admire?

Pray

Come, Holy Spirit, intercede for us with sighs too deep for words. Enter our hearts too easily grown cold and stir them into passion. The task is not nearly done. The future stretches out before us and God's future claims us anew.

Part Two

Reconciliation and Renewal

So when you are offering your gift at the altar, if you remember that your brother or sister has something against you, leave your gift there before the altar and go; first be reconciled to your brother or sister, and then come and offer your gift. Come to terms quickly with your accuser while you are on the way to court with him, or your accuser may hand you over to the judge, and the judge to the guard, and you will be thrown into prison.

—MATTHEW 5:23–25

O ur technology is far advanced, our clothing styles are different, and none of us really speaks Aramaic anymore. But some things are exactly the same as they were in the first century. We still experience anger and animosity, we still do things that break the bonds of our communities. And in the gospel, Jesus still reminds us, even today, that we are called to be friends. Reconciliation and renewal need to happen in our families, our communities, and the world.

Sacred Conversation

Thus the Lord said, "The cry of the Israelites has now come to me; I have also seen how the Egyptians oppress them. So come, I will send you to Pharaoh to bring my people, the Israelites, out of Egypt." But Moses said to God, "Who am I, that I should go to Pharaoh and bring the Israelites out of Egypt?" And God said, "I will be with you; and this shall be the sign for you that it is I who sent you: when you have brought the people out of Egypt, you shall worship God on this mountain."
—EXODUS 3:9–12

Possibly no chapter in this book needs the back-story told more than this one.

The story that follows is based on a sermon that was preached at Trinity United Church of Christ in one of Chicago's poorest neighborhoods. The church was founded in 1961, a small, struggling congregation served by some of the United Church of Christ's finest African American preachers. In March of 1972, a young minister by the name of Jeremiah Wright came to serve Trinity. His eloquent preaching style and his commitment to justice and the poor, along with his training in community organizing, brought Trinity alive. The congregation grew to five thousand members and the neighborhood blossomed with improved schools and lively neighborhood organizations. Rev. Wright attracted successful blacks to the congregation, which became the parish of choice for upward-bound, socially conscious African American professionals. Among them were Barack and Michelle Obama. Their two daughters were baptized by Rev. Wright.

Fast-forward to 2008. Barack Obama was in the midst of a campaign that resulted in his historic win as the first African American president of the United States. Those who knew Rev. Wright, as I did, were not surprised that his challenging preaching would find its way into the campaign's media coverage. But few would have predicted—I surely did not—that his preaching would become the center of one of the most contentious issues facing Obama's campaign.

Before Barack Obama's membership in Trinity became a campaign liability, Reverend Wright declared that his time had come to retire. He named as his successor the Reverend Dr. Otis Moss III. Young Otis was well known to me and to my family. His father, the Reverend Dr. Otis Moss, Jr., was Cleveland's most highly respected African American pastor. Time and space do not allow me to tell you the many ways the Moss and Campbell families were intertwined. Both Rev. Moss, Jr., and I worked for Martin Luther King, Jr. Though Dr. Moss's involvement was at a much higher level than mine, I was one of a few whites who supported the election of Carl B. Stokes as mayor of Cleveland in 1964. My support for candidate Stokes came about as a result of my involvement with the National Council of Churches' backing of a voter registration campaign headed by Martin Luther King, Jr. Dr. Moss knew the depth of my personal sacrifice for the civil rights movement, and years later he supported my daughter, Jane, when she ran for mayor of Cleveland in 2001.

Later, in 2002, young Otis Moss III came to the Chautauqua Institution at my invitation. He was one of the youngest preachers to proclaim the message of faith from that national ecumenical pulpit. His preaching, eloquent and prophetic, was awarded the coveted Harrington Prize, which recognizes people early in their careers who show exemplary promise in ministry. That honor, combined with his talent, put him on the national stage and caught the attention of

Jeremiah Wright at Trinity UCC. So the Moss and Campbell families became more deeply intertwined.

But all was not peaceful, especially when Jane ran for reelection in 2005 and Dr. Moss chose to support neither Jane nor her opponent. The issue of race once again challenged treasured relationships. But beyond the disappointment of Dr. Moss's non-support for Jane, there remained a treasured relationship.

In 2008, young Otis was caught in the middle of election politics. In the wake of the furor over Rev. Wright's preaching, Obama resigned his membership from Trinity and Jeremiah Wright was daily in the news. Otis was caught between demonstrators outside the church and tension within. So when Otis called and asked me to preach on May 25, the theme that Sunday was "A Conversation on Race." I readily accepted his invitation and was joined by my daughter, now the former mayor of Cleveland, and by young Otis's mother and father.

Saying yes to the assignment took a touch of courage, and the scripture that seemed most fit for the moment was the story of a reluctant Moses (Exodus 3:9–12), called by God to serve. Moses's hesitation seemed so fitting as I wrestled with these questions: why me, why this subject, why here, why now?

So I began my sermon by sharing some of my own history in the civil rights movement and the way my involvement threatened my husband's career.

▪

It was 1964, and the world was turning itself upside down. President John F. Kennedy had just been assassinated, President Lyndon Johnson had signed the Civil Rights Act into law, and a hundred thousand U.S. soldiers were on the ground in Vietnam. I was living in Ohio, and you'd think I might have been sheltered from the turmoil—I was a young mother of three spirited children, and the wife of a soon-to-be successful corporate lawyer. But my world was turned upside down, too.

In the prosperous Cleveland suburb of Shaker Heights, Ohio, the ground beneath us was trembling. The secure, well-to-do pillars of the Cleveland community were confronted with new neighbors—lawyers, teachers, doctors, dentists who also happened to be African American. Martin Luther King, Jr.'s, voice rang out across the land, but mostly from a distance. As long as King's words were not spoken in their backyard, Shaker residents found King's words prophetic. The churches, from the pulpit, preached equality—but the response from the pews was mixed. There were those who responded to the gospel call to action and those who believed the status quo was the way the world was meant to be.

Encouraged by the preachers' words and by what seemed to be social acceptance, black Americans and their supporters began to dream aloud of an America where political and economic power would be shared. Just eight miles down the highway from Shaker Heights, Cleveland's black community eyed the Stokes brothers—Louis and Carl—as potential candidates for office, and Martin Luther King, Jr., took interest in what was going on in Cleveland. As the possibility of Cleveland's election of the first-ever black mayor seemed likely, as Shaker's all-white neighborhood began to change, conversations about race were the order of the day. For white people concerned about how to preserve their privileged status and hold their majority power, the conversations were characterized by fear, guilt, resentment, and uncertainty—and sometimes by outright bigotry. But for others, the call to integrate seemed right.

Our church, Heights Christian Church, in the heart of Shaker Heights, had just called a young new minister, a Yale graduate whose education seemed properly prestigious for this privileged white congregation. The Reverend Dr. Albert Pennybacker brought the message of justice, freedom, and equality. He was a pastor with the soul of a reformer and the carefree courage of the young, and he took our congregation on a journey from which there would be no return. Along with my church, I entered a life-defining struggle, and life as I had known it was to be forever changed. My faith suddenly took on meaning and purpose.

I had grown up in a family of faith. It was a way of life for me, but my faith had not required me to make any sacrifices. I prayed, I went to church, I taught Sunday school, I was the president of the Women's Society—time-consuming, worthwhile activities but not ones that put me at odds with family or friends or compromised a successful life. My entry into the world of racial justice as an active, marching, declared antiracist unnerved my mother, my friends, and especially my young husband, whose law firm favored wives who were dignified, quiet, and accomplished in the social graces. Quiet I was not, and my subsequent work with the civil rights movement did not jibe with the expectations of the managing members of the firm.

My faith took on a passion that stirred my soul. I had decisions to make that would rock my marriage. The struggle for justice gave meaning to my otherwise predictable, secure, conformable life. I walked with Martin Luther King, Jr., and my children walked with me—which posed problems for a marriage that was less stable than I had chosen to believe.

I began to see that genuine faith is costly—it is cross-bearing. To choose life is almost always painful.

As the civil rights struggles in our community and across the country intensified, our church became more divided, our young minister became more active in the civil rights movement, and his teaching and preaching became more profound and more important. He reminded us that race is not a sociological issue but a theological one. That simple truth has informed my decisions from that day to this. This radical reordering of the civil rights struggle placed it, for me, squarely in the realm of the sacred.

My daughter, Jane, was eleven years old in 1964, when Martin Luther King, Jr., spearheaded a voter-registration campaign in Cleveland, focused on registering African American voters for the campaign of Carl B. Stokes as the first African American mayor of a major American city. All three of my children worked on the campaign, stuffing envelopes, distributing brochures, answering phones—and coming face to face with the bitterness of those whose identity was threatened by the possibility of a black mayor. Jane looked around and saw the swell of emotions and the storm of vitriol, and asked, "Why would anyone want to be mayor in the midst of such turmoil?"

I recall Carl Stokes sitting in our living room for a meeting, responding, "Jane, someday there may be a first woman who will be mayor of Cleveland. Who is mayor of Cleveland may make more difference to the lives of the poor than any other single thing that can happen, because of the decisions that he or she can make."

Carl Stokes narrowly won that election. And nearly forty years later, in 2002, Jane became Cleveland's first woman mayor. When people ask her why she chose this path, she answers simply and humbly that she believes it is what faith had called her to do with her life.

God calls each of us to holy action and the work of reconciliation, but like many who have gone before us, we tend to hesitate. Consider the biblical story of Moses. I like him because he is so much like us. When God called him to lead the Israelites out of slavery in Egypt, he did his best to avoid the job. First he tried anxiety: "What if they don't believe?" he whined. "What if they don't listen to me?" (Exodus 4:1). God didn't buy it.

His next tactic: "Why me?" He was slow of speech and slow of tongue, he quickly pointed out to God (Exodus 4:10). God didn't buy that, either.

Finally, he tried to pass the ball to his brother: "Pick Aaron!" he suggested (Exodus 4:13). But God was still not persuaded. God chose Moses, and Moses was to respond. God required action, not excuses.

Martin Luther King, Jr., put it like this in his speech at Riverside Church in New York on April 4, 1967: "We must move past indecision to action.... If we do not act we shall surely be dragged down the long, dark, and shameful corridors of time reserved for those who possess power without compassion, might without morality, and strength without sight."[1]

Whatever our time or place—whether it is ancient Egypt, contemporary America, or anything in between—God calls us and God expects us to respond.

Sometimes, the most important thing—and the most difficult thing—God calls us to is conversation. In the words of Michael Kinnamon, general secretary of the National Council of Churches, as he addressed the Aquinas Institute of Theology in St. Louis in 2008, "We are God's children only, but we are not God's only children." None of us can claim exclusive rights to God's magnificent, inclusive love. God's love is for every person. We do not take God's love to another; God's love is already there. Privilege does not exist. God loves us all.

That is the root of the sacred conversation about race.

The conversation about racial justice must continue today. Though Barack Obama is the first black man to serve as president of our country, we still have unfinished business to attend to. Blacks and whites continue to wrestle with how to trust one another. At this moment in our national history, can we, as people of faith, afford *not* to continue the dialogue?

If anyone thinks this is easy, they have never been in the eye of the storm. After all, we are called to take part in a profound conversation, and then to step out boldly in faith and find our way together to the Beloved Community that Dr. King envisioned. It was justice that took him to the mountaintop, and it was the fear that justice might succeed that ended his life far too soon. The love he preached was too threatening for too many. Not everyone wanted to embrace it.

On April 3, 1968, Dr. King visited Memphis, where he delivered what would be the last speech of his life, which came to be known as the "I've Been to the Mountaintop" address. The next evening, as he prepared for another event, he was shot to death on the balcony of his hotel. He was just thirty-nine years old.

King's journey was both sacred and sacrificial. His life raised for us this question: what is the cost of truly sacred conversation about a reality that has divided this nation since its earliest days?

We need not think, of course, that the struggle for racial justice belongs exclusively to our country. It is a global struggle, one shared particularly by South Africa, with its history of apartheid. Apartheid—an Afrikaans word for "separateness"—was the racial segregation policy enforced in South Africa, under which the civil rights of black inhabitants of the country were restricted while white domination was maintained. The violent struggle against apartheid steadily grew until the system was overthrown in 1994.

Beyers Naudé's experience raises an equally important question: what is the cost of *not* having that conversation? His is a poignant story of a young white man marked for success, who risked everything for justice—and paid the price. As a young man, bright and articulate, he was a rising star in South African society and in the Dutch Reformed Church. He presided over a large and prestigious congregation in the suburbs of Cape Town, the second most populous city in South Africa as well as its legislative capital, and he was elected to a select group of young men called the Broederbond, the *crème de la crème* of South African society and the church. They were the architects and defenders of the apartheid system.

Beyers Naudé was marked for leadership, possibly even as the president of his country. But his "perfect" life made him uneasy. He felt like a blind man refusing to see the reality of those around him. One day, one of his black servants got word that his wife was dying in childbirth. Despite the man's protests, Beyers Naudé put the man in his own car and rushed, with his own doctor, to the township where the man lived.

Beyers Naudé had never been to the township before. The man's wife lived, the child died, and Beyers Naudé's blindness ended. He saw with his own eyes the devastating and impoverishing effect that apartheid had on the blacks of his country. What he saw forced him to see the system of apartheid in a whole new way, through the eyes of his faith. The eyes of faith, after all, do not see the world in the same way that others do. The eyes of faith, seeing pain and problems and injustice, cannot ignore the reality. Perhaps Beyers Naudé's story especially affected me because it so strongly paralleled my own.

But Beyers Naudé paid dearly for his new vision. Because he dared to speak against the government, against apartheid, he was defrocked by his church, stripped of his robe and his clergy credentials. He was put under house arrest and ostracized by his friends and his government because to speak against apartheid was to break the law. Yet as his worldly fortunes dwindled, his spirit soared. His deepened faith had made him whole, and he became one of his nation's most ardent and effective anti-apartheid activists.

As a white man, he knew he would never play a leadership role in the country that he helped to free. In fact the thought never occurred to him, for he knew his task was to prepare the way for black leadership. Beyers Naudé became director of the South African Council of Churches, but he vowed to stay only until black leadership was identified. The black man who took his place was the young Desmond Tutu, a South African cleric and activist who rose to worldwide fame during the 1980s as an opponent of apartheid. Tutu was the first black South African Anglican archbishop of Cape Town and the second South African to be awarded the Nobel Peace Prize. Beyers Naudé had prepared a place for him.

Through the years, Beyers Naudé had kept his ties to the Broederbond and when the time came to negotiate a peace between F. W. de Klerk, the last white leader of South Africa, and Nelson Mandela, the first black leader, Beyers Naudé played a major role. Because his eyes had been opened to a world of unity, the world was blessed with a peacemaker and a whole nation was changed. He was a privileged white man who responded to a divine call with acts of love. Some would say he gave up everything. He would counter that he gained his life.

Beyers Naudé; Martin Luther King, Jr.; and a host of others moved past sacred conversation into the realm of holy action. But conversation is where they started, and that is our clear call today. Though we who live in the United States have elected a black president, problems of race have not disappeared, and the need for reconciliation is as great as ever—but sacred conversation seems to have dwindled even as the anger and division and vitriol of cable news channels has become louder.

Martin Luther King, Jr.; Carl Stokes; Beyers Naudé—and certainly Moses—these people heard the call, started the sacred conversation, and followed through with holy action. That's what all of us, as people of faith, are called to do—in our homes, our workplaces, our churches: Listen. Talk. Do. Talk isn't cheap. Talk is holy. The work of reconciliation depends on it.

REFLECT

When has your faith led you to a decision that was both professionally and personally costly? How was it life-changing? How was it renewing?

PRAY

Loving God,
  Your reach is broad,
  Your vision bold,
  Your love deeper than the deepest ocean,
  Wider than the universe we know.
Forgive us the limits of our loving.
Forgive us the timidity of our vision.

Forgive us our special pleading,
    Reserving you for us and our kind.
        Lord, have mercy.

Eternal God,
    Your image lies in the hearts of all people.
    You have given life to us and to people
        Whose ways are different from ours,
        Whose faiths are foreign to us,
        Whose languages are unintelligible to us.
    Forgive us for claiming that we alone
        have favor in your eyes.
        Lord, have mercy.

Creator God,
    You set the stars in the midnight sky,
    You brought light into deepest darkness,
    You brushed away the shadows where fear grows,
        Where bigotry and war and hatred are fed.
    You sent us a child and love was born.
    Peace was made possible.
    Forgive us, O God,
        The fears that reside in the deep recesses of our
        broken hearts.
    Help us to recognize you in the words of truth,
        The things of beauty, the actions of love around us.
        Lord, have mercy.

Almighty God,
    We are your grateful people,
        And we are reminded that in compassion God
        forgives us.
    Enable us to turn from the way of violence and death.
    Show us how to choose and cherish life.

I say to you in the name of Jesus the Christ,
 You are forgiven.
Receive the great promise:
 The past is over and gone. All things will be made new.
  Amen.

Prodigals and the Path to Peace

The son said to him, "Father, I have sinned against heaven and before you; I am no longer worthy to be called your son."
—LUKE 15:21

O*nce upon a time there was a prodigal son.* Everybody knows the parable about forgiveness and reconciliation that Jesus told. It's in the Bible, and it's played out every day in somebody's family, in somebody's community, all around the world. It's a family drama, a very human story that pulls at our hearts and at our experience just as much now as it did twenty centuries ago.

It goes like this: There was a family with two sons. The elder was a model child who stayed home to work the family farm; the younger one asked for his inheritance and headed out for a more glamorous life. But when his money and friends ran out, the prodigal came back home, humbled and remorseful, and asked his father for a job in his fields. Instead of punishing him, his father greeted him with joy, killed the fatted calf, and threw a welcome-home party.

It has always been easy to put myself into this parable. I was a dutiful first child with a sister who tested my parents at every turn. I did what I was told. I was a good girl; I did my homework and got good grades and helped with the household chores. I didn't give my parents anxiety attacks—and deep down, I guess, I expected some appreciation for all my efforts. My sister, on the other hand (whose missionary work, I've often said, was penance for her early days of misbehavior), kept my parents constantly on edge. If the curfew was midnight (and it was in those days), I would be home five minutes early, while Betty would roll in about half past twelve. Betty got her share of lectures, but my mother was always so relieved to see her, she would greet her with a hug and a prayer of gratitude for her safety. I was glad she got home in one piece, but I confess that, like the elder child in the parable, I was a bit resentful. I identified totally with the pious older brother in the story. I had been a good child, and there did not seem to be much reward in being good when all the attention went to my sister. It just didn't seem quite right.

In 1998, the country was rocked by a scandal involving a relationship between President Bill Clinton and a White House intern, Monica Lewinsky, leading to the president's impeachment. When a bipartisan group of senators asked me to preach to them on the theme of reconciliation, the parable of the prodigal son is the text I chose for my sermon. This bipartisan, interfaith group of senators saw clearly the need for reconciliation if the nation's business was to move forward. And the nation wanted to hear the president confess. They wanted to hear him admit, as the prodigal son had, "I have sinned against heaven and before you" (Luke 15:21).

In this parable, we usually focus on the father's forgiveness, which is instantly and wholeheartedly offered to his younger son. But the parable is also about confession and the process of reconciliation. Even as we long for a confession from the wayward one, we need to confess our own unworthiness too. It's the saintly—maybe even self-righteous—older brother who has difficulty being reconciled. The wayward younger brother confesses his sins with sincere remorse, and the father forgives him before the words are even uttered. The older brother, though, feels he has nothing to confess.

With the party plans in full swing, the older boy, in a fit of pique, confronts the father, demanding, "What is all this music and dancing and carrying on? This boy, this son of yours, who gave us so much difficulty—you've *embraced* him?"

The older brother's reaction is totally human. I know now, even as I knew as a child, that it was right for my parents to embrace my wayward sister. And looking back, I realize she really wasn't all that wayward—and she was, after all, a member of the family. She was loved and treasured even when she exasperated my parents. In the parable, the father replies to the jealous older brother, "Son, you are always with me, and all that is mine is yours. But we had to celebrate and rejoice, because this brother of yours was dead and has come to life" (Luke 15:31–32).

The father acted out of his understanding of forgiveness and of family. He prepared a feast, brought out the party clothes, and put a ring on this younger son's finger. When the boy protested, "I am no longer worthy to be called your son," the father warmly welcomed him home anyway. The text does not say for sure, but it hints that the wayward son was reconciled to God, to his father, and finally to his older brother.

Yet in many ways the older brother was the one most in need of reconciliation to his God. The younger brother's salvation was in his confession—his mistakes were so clear to him that it was a simple matter to admit his unworthiness. He claimed for himself no sense of privilege; his only claim was his need for forgiveness. He became, as Paul writes in his second letter to the Corinthians, "a new creation" (2 Corinthians 5:17). But the older brother had to come to grips with the reality that he, too, needed forgiveness. His goodness, which had become his pride, his birthright, his sense of privilege, had to give way for him to be able to lay claim to the generous gift of love. This, really, is what the story is all about.

Pope John Paul II, in "Reconciliation and Penance," spoke about this parable in a very helpful way:

> If the parable is read from the point of view of the other
> son, it portrays the situation of the human family,
> divided by forms of selfishness. It throws light on the
> difficulty involved in satisfying the desire and longing
> for one reconciled and united family. It therefore
> reminds us of the need for a profound transformation of
> hearts through the rediscovery of the Father's mercy
> and through victory over misunderstanding and over
> hostility among brothers and sisters.[1]

The parable of the prodigal son throws light on the difficulty
involved in satisfying the desire and longing for one reconciled and
united family. It reminds us of the need for a profound transforma-
tion of hearts through the rediscovery of God's mercy and through
victory over misunderstanding and hostility among the larger family
of brothers and sisters.

It may not be easy for those of us who are the "good" and dutiful
members of the family to believe we are all loved equally by God, but
that is our only hope for reconciliation and for peace. This was the
consistent message that Desmond Tutu, the Anglican archbishop of
Cape Town, South Africa, spoke as he worked against apartheid.
Archbishop Tutu is a tiny man, except when he preaches—then he is
very tall indeed. I remember his speaking to the General Board of the
National Council of Churches while I was the general secretary.
Desmond was looking out at an audience of three or four thousand
people who were at the gathering, saying, "God loves you." And the
people there must have thought, "We've paid to have him come all
the way here from South Africa to say that? We know that!" And then
he stopped, looked at his listeners, and declared, "God loves everyone." That's the tough part. How ironic—the wayward younger
brother who wasted his father's money is also God's child.

John Hope Franklin, a wise man who chaired President Clinton's
panel on racism, once attended a dinner party at Jesse Jackson's

home. I also attended this party. One of the guests asked Dr. Franklin the provocative question whether he thought the nation should apologize for slavery.

Dr. Franklin was a courteous, well-bred man. I recall that he was very quiet for a while and then he answered, "I do not intend to put my time into that. I won't do that because it is not slavery that perpetuates racism in this nation. It is white people's sense of privilege, of entitlement, of an exaggerated sense of self-worth that is the problem. For the nation's wounds to be healed, for equality to be realized, white people must recognize their sense of privilege that grants them special status and denies equality to others."

In the same way, the self-righteous older brother in the parable teaches all who arrogantly claim their birthright that they too need forgiveness.

The Truth and Reconciliation Commission established in South Africa following the fall of apartheid, the system of racial segregation that was in place in that country between 1948 and 1994, is a good example of this need for forgiveness. South Africa's black community had every right to be angry, perhaps even to hate, for their lives had been made a living hell. Their children had been denied their God-given potential. They had been damaged by the cruel system of apartheid, created by the government and sanctioned by the church. But Nelson Mandela and Desmond Tutu saw a more excellent way.

The Truth and Reconciliation Commission was born of Mandela's and Tutu's belief that for the nation to heal, truth had to replace the falsehoods of apartheid. South African blacks had suffered unspeakable threats, indignities, and mistreatment, and for years their stories were dismissed as lies. For there to be peace it was important for South African whites to admit to the atrocities that had cost blacks their very lives. The commission existed as a place where truth could be told, crimes admitted, confessions heard, forgiveness requested and granted, and reconciliation made possible. Both Tutu and Mandela believed that punishing the criminal would not alone create a climate of reconciliation; rather, it was important that crimes be admitted and the truth be told.

One example of the effectiveness of this process is the true story of Frank Chikane, a personal friend whom I came to know because of his involvement in the ecumenical movement, and who followed Desmond Tutu as general secretary of the South African Council of Churches and then served as chief of staff to Thabo Mbeki, president of South Africa following Mandela. As Frank wrestled with his decision to leave his place of exile in England and return to South Africa in the heat of the apartheid struggle, he sought refuge in my home in New York City, where he could safely reflect with colleagues on this decision. He did indeed return home, where he was from the beginning a target of the pro-apartheid faction. He openly accused them of trying to kill him by inserting poison into his clothes during the dry-cleaning process. The charge was seen as so ridiculous that it was dismissed out of hand.

But as is often the case, truth will have its day. Frank's wife was studying African languages at the University of Wisconsin, and when Frank came to visit her he became critically ill. He was rushed to the hospital, where he miraculously recovered quickly. This happened twice more in the space of two days. Finally, poison experts were called in and found that he became ill when he went home and put on his clothes and healed when they were removed. His clothes had indeed been poisoned. No one believed him until the U.S. doctors proved him to be a truth teller. Those who did the poisoning confessed before the Truth and Reconciliation Commission. Truth was told and honored— the power of truth was greater than the power of punishment.

The sacred insists that truth must be told. Reconciliation will not happen unless we speak the truth of our fears, our hopes, and our transgressions to one another. This is the root of the South African Truth and Reconciliation Commission: Truth must be spoken before forgiveness can be made real. Forgiveness must be offered before reconciliation is possible.

The power of confession cannot be overstated. Our equality before God may not be easy. It may not be easy for those of us who are older brothers or older sisters, but it is in fact our only hope for peace.

Reconciliation may be a gift from God, but our calling is to respond to the generosity of this gift by loving one another, especially those who are difficult to love. The unattractive qualities we see in both the older brother and the younger brother are everywhere, but so is the capacity to forgive and to rise above our foolish ways.

The search for reconciliation takes us out of ourselves and focuses us on the gifts and graces of the other. That, of course, is what the father asked of the older brother when he said, "Your brother was lost and has been found" (Luke 15:32). The father was really saying, "Step out of yourself. Take a look at your brother. See what it is that he has to offer his family." The idea that God loves us all hardly seems fair. But if we fail to believe this deep down, if we continue to hold grudges against one another, or consider ourselves superior, the possibility for a peaceful society diminishes.

I was asked to be an honorary election monitor (our task was, by our presence, to ensure a free and fair election) during the elections that made Nelson Mandela the first black South African to serve as president of his country. There were four on our team, each from a different country, but we were overshadowed by the most significant member of our group, Kenneth Kaunda, the former president of Zambia.

To help you understand Kaunda's story, I have to insert another short story. The president of South Africa, Thabo Mbeki, whom I knew when he was in exile in Zambia, told me this account. His father was a law partner of Mandela, and when Mandela and Thabo's father were about to be jailed, his father gathered the family together and took them to the border of Zambia and South Africa, with the police right behind them. His father said, "Run, Thabo, run."

Thabo ran, and it was Kaunda who gave the family refuge. As president of Zambia, Kaunda was despised in South Africa because he hid the enemy. His country gave refuge to the African National

Congress, which worked for the rights of black Africans, long before it became an acceptable organization.

During all the years of apartheid, Kaunda had not been allowed in South Africa, so when our monitoring team went into Zululand, word went out about Kaunda's presence in the area. When people saw him, they cried, "It's Kaunda, it's Kaunda," over and over, like a mantra. They wanted to see him close up, to touch him. He had to have a bodyguard because so many people wanted to see him.

We ended up in a local Anglican church with a congregation that had been engaged in a round-the-clock vigil throughout the entire time of the election. We had been sitting there, in about the third row, for a half-hour when, suddenly, there was a commotion. I saw the bodyguards move closer to Kaunda, who was sitting at the edge of the aisle.

An agitated white man came forward, and the guards let him sit beside Kaunda. We couldn't hear the conversation, but we saw the white man weeping. He spoke briefly with Kaunda, then left.

Later that night Kaunda told us about the conversation in the church. "The man who came to me said, 'President Kaunda, I am a member of the South African police. My job was to hunt you down and kill you. Tonight, in this church, I come to you, and I ask your forgiveness in order that I might become a part of the new South Africa.'" And Kaunda had looked at him and said, "Let it be so."

Therein lies reconciliation, healing, and hope. In forgiveness lies the only way to peace.

REFLECT

What experiences have you had that help you to identify with the struggle for justice? Have you ever been denied justice because truth was withheld?

PRAY

God of love and life,

God of pardon,

God of vision,

Day after day—the world around—we pray your kingdom come, your will be done on earth as it is in heaven.

You call us to live out your kingdom vision here where we live and love and work and worship.

Forgive us when we focus only on heaven and fail to work toward your kingdom here on earth.

Lord, have mercy.

God, you created all that is, all that will ever be—every tree, every animal, every plant, every child.

Your creation goes beyond our capacity to know and understand worlds beyond our world.

You have carefully created a kingdom that requires interdependence.

Forgive us for our inability to see life whole, to live as a precious part of a magnificent and peaceable kingdom.

Forgive us our human penchant for division.

Lord, have mercy.

Jesus, facing death on the cross, you prayed not for your own life but for our unity.

You prayed that we might be ONE so that the world might believe your message.

You knew that our boundaries and walls would never be a witness to your love.

Forgive us the division between our churches and our nations, between the races, between young and old, women and men.

Lord, have mercy.

Loving God, you created us for community.
You filled our earth with all good things.
You created us with the capacity to share, to be open to all.
You created a world without boundaries.
Forgive us for the barriers built by human hands, human ingenuity.
Remind us of our moments when walls came down and peace broke out.
Love us until your kingdom comes.
Lord, have mercy.

Lord God, your holy scriptures sing with your kingdom vision, where weak hands are strengthened,
   feeble knees made firm,
   fearful hearts made strong,
   the eyes of the blind opened and the ears of the deaf unstopped.
When we fail to reach for this vision of a better world for all your creation,
Forgive us for breaking your heart.
Lord, have mercy.

God, by your love, celebrated in your Word,
   seen in your Son,
   brought near by your Spirit,
Take from us what we need carry no longer
   so that we may be free again
   to choose to serve you
   and be served by each other.
To all and to each in the community,
God pronounces pardon and grants us the right to begin again.
Thanks be to God.
Amen.

For Such a
Time as This

*After that I will go to the king, though it
is against the law; and if I perish, I perish.*
—ESTHER 4:16

T he choices we make are a picture of our lives.
My granddaughter Katie asked me a difficult question:
"Gramsie," she demanded, "what does it feel like to have more years
behind you than ahead of you?"

I took a deep breath and realized that she was right. I *did* have
more years behind me than ahead of me. (And I was also glad I wasn't
fifteen again!) I thought about the fact that we are a composite of the
choices that we have made and, when we can look backward, we can
begin to understand these choices.

I don't mean the little daily choices about what jacket to wear or
what to cook for supper, but the choices that give our life timbre, sub-
stance, direction, and meaning. The time comes for every single human
being when we make a formative choice. In my experience a choice
like that happens only after wrestling and uncertainty, and only after at
least one person has advised me against it. And always it is fraught
with a heaping measure of risk and the scary absence of security.

I had a moment like that in 1999, when I decided to accompany a
group of delegates to Belgrade, which was being bombed by NATO

forces. During the 1990s, under the leadership of Slobodan Milosevic, Kosovo, a province in southern Yugoslavia, had been experiencing violent conflict between two ethnic groups, the Serbs and the Albanians. As atrocities against Albanians increased and hundreds of thousands of people were forced from their homes, President Bill Clinton demanded that President Milosevic allow a peacekeeping force into the region. When Milosevic refused, the United States and its European allies launched a bombing attack against the country.

It was in the midst of this conflict that several American soldiers were captured by the Yugoslavian military, and our group went there to bring them back home. Everyone thought it was a crazy idea, including my children. "Mother, you're going *where?*" they demanded, ganging up on me. "Don't you think you have this backward?" my son Paul inquired. "Don't you understand that sons go to war and their mothers stay home and pray for them?"

We went because Patriarch Pavle, forty-fourth patriarch of the Serbian Orthodox Church, asked us to come and stand with him. Patriarch Pavle had led the Serbian Orthodox Church through its post-Communist revival and called for peace and reconciliation during the terrible Balkan conflicts of the 1990s. We were a hodgepodge group: led by the Reverend Jesse Jackson, we included Leonid Kishkovsky, the Serbian Orthodox bishop from the United States; Bishop Kodic Mitrophan and Bishop Irinej Dobrijevic from the Serbian Orthodox Church; Bishop Dimitrios Couchell of the Greek Orthodox Church; Nazir Udin Khaja, president of the board of the American Muslim Council; Steven Bennett Jacobs, a rabbi from Los Angeles; Bishop Marshall L. Meadors of the United Methodist Church in Jackson, Mississippi; the Reverend Raymond Glen Helmick, a Jesuit scholar and conflict-resolution specialist from Boston College; Landrum Bolling, a Quaker and director of Mercy Corps; Rod Blagojevich, a congressman from Illinois; and me.

The United States government went to great lengths to discourage us from going on our mission. Just six hours before we were to begin our journey—by one plane to Germany and another to Croatia, then by bus and by foot, over land, from Croatia into Belgrade—we were summoned to the White House for a briefing with National Security Advisor Sandy Berger, who offered us stern and discomfiting words. "We want you to know that despite your presence the bombing will not only continue while you are there," he said, "it will intensify and you will be in danger. And we doubt that you will get the prisoners out. We want you to know that we will do nothing to protect you."

With that grim warning, we were dismissed, and the twelve of us prayed together, then talked about what we would do. It was clear there was going to be danger. As the only woman in the delegation, I felt compelled to rein in the cowboys. "Gentlemen," I said, "let's not play *High Noon* here. This mission is very dangerous. Let's reduce the testosterone level just a bit." They were not scared. I had to be scared for them. But we all had to ponder the purpose of this mission to Belgrade. Why was it worth risking life and limb? Why was it worth giving enormous anxiety to our families? Before boarding the plane, we had to have some very serious conversation.

And when we did, we realized that we had to go. We realized that people in Croatia needed our support. We knew, from the power and safety of our nation, that we had to go and stand with the Serbians in the weakness and danger and desperation of theirs. We knew we had to make a choice on behalf of justice.

Maybe, in the end, my choice to go on the Belgrade trip was a little bit like the Hebrew girl Esther's choice to face the king and seek justice for her people—though she knew she could die. But with faith in her God she did it anyway. "I will go to the king," she said, "and if I perish, I perish" (Esther 4:16).

The Hebrew Bible story of Esther takes place during the exile of the Jews in Babylonia, in about the sixth century BCE, in the court of the Persian king. When the king asks his wife to display her beauty to all his guests, she refuses, so the angry king banishes her and looks for another queen. He chooses a young girl, Esther, who—unknown to the king—is Jewish. Soon, when Esther's uncle, a palace gatekeeper, tells her about a plot against all the Jews in the city, Esther goes to the king to report the plan, even though entering his room uninvited is a capital offense. But she takes the chance, thwarts the plot, and saves the lives of her people.

Esther made a choice that was both life-giving and life-threatening. By deciding to go before the king, she risked her life. But by deciding to risk her life, she opened the possibility of saving her people.

Esther has always been one of my biblical heroines, inspiring me with her courage and her audacity. She made the choice she knew was right, trusting in God, even as she knew the outcome was not guaranteed. As a woman of faith, how could I not try to do the same? In the end, of course, we boarded that plane, we got on that bus, and, like a bold little contingent of Esthers, we made our way to Slobodan Milosevic. The so-called butcher of the Balkans treated us to a lengthy sermon on Serbian history, and Jesse Jackson responded with an equally lengthy exposition on the private, humanitarian nature of our mission and on the value of trying to break a stalemate between the West and Yugoslavia. We also appealed to Milosevic's media savvy, suggesting that a prisoner release would be a smart move. Make a gesture, we urged again and again. Then we'll see what happens.

For four hours we went back and forth. We made our best case, and then we trooped out.

Several hours later, Jesse Jackson and I were invited to the private residence of Yugoslav Foreign Minister Zivadin Jovanovic. "I'm pleased to tell you," he announced, "that President Milosevic has issued a decree today releasing the three soldiers."

We were left alone with this news. Jesse wept with disbelief. There was no bravado, no claiming of victory, only thanks to a God who had answered our unspoken prayers. We went back to the hotel and told our traveling companions. There was no rejoicing, simply quiet awe and thanksgiving. We readied ourselves to be at the jail by five in the morning, packed and ready to leave town quickly![1]

I will never forget the scene as we stood in the military installation where Staff Sergeant Andrew Ramirez, Staff Sergeant Christopher Stone, and Specialist Steven Gonzales were being held. A staff member ran through the procedure for prisoners to be handed over. The young men were to come down with their hands behind their backs, he explained. They would have no laces in their shoes and, until the papers were signed, they would keep their hands behind their backs.

Before the ink had dried on those signatures, Reverend Jackson turned to these young men, who had been in solitary confinement for forty days and forty nights. "Gentlemen, gentlemen," he said, "Take your hands from behind your backs. You are free men."

That moment was life-changing, not only for these three soldiers and their families, but to those of us who witnessed it. Much later, Jesse Jackson was asked, "When did you believe that you would get the soldiers out?"

"I knew we would get them out," he responded, "when we decided to go."

That choice was the watershed moment. From the moment we arrived, we shared in Yugoslavia's danger. Right outside our hotel, a building was blown up, shattering the glass of our hotel's windows. We knew that our willingness to enter into the reality of the Yugoslavian people, to experience the air raid sirens, the bombings, the terror, gave credibility to our caring and gave peace a chance.

When we met with Patriarch Pavle, the leader of the Serbian Church, he expressed his gratitude. "Thank you for coming," he said. "Thank you for placing yourselves under bombs that your own government has sent. Thank you for placing yourself in harm's way. Thank you for giving us the courage to defeat this dictator."

To many people, our little delegation looked like a ragtag bunch who had made a crazy decision to go to Yugoslavia, a country under the thumbs of a ruthless dictator not much different from the king of Esther's day. Yet as I look back, I see our delegation not as people who changed a moment of history, but as flawed human beings who responded to God's call, who were there when God needed them.

People like Queen Esther, people like you and me—we are chosen by God not because we can transcend the dilemmas and challenges of human nature, but because we understand that we can continue to be the messengers of divine demand despite our weaknesses. Our lives are not devoid of blemishes and problems; our voices are not protected from wavering and cracking. But in our weaknesses lie the ability to speak with compassion and sensitivity, to respond to the turmoil and twists of history. It is within this very humanness that is embedded the challenge to remain obedient to God's calling.

It's Esther's humanity, not her perfection, that is instructive for us, that shows us how to learn from her choice. First, her choice was characterized by compassion, risk, danger, sacrifice. It was directed not toward herself but toward somebody else. Knowing that personal pain, loss of status, and even death were potential results, she still made her choice.

Esther's decision required absolute honesty. God had greater claim on her than her loyalty to the king, despite all his wealth and power. Esther was God's woman, and God had hold of her. It was this above all that gave her wisdom.

And Esther's choice was informed by her ability to read the signs of the times. She did not allow her privileged status to mask the reality of the suffering around her. She faced the truth and responded with courage.

Esther risked death but chose life, and therein lies the message, a message repeated again and again in the Bible. Does not Jesus in fact tell us that to find our life we must lose it (Matthew 10:39; 16:25)? The gospel message is clear: faithfulness to Jesus's message requires that we be willing to lay down our lives for our friends (John 15:12–13).

We know that Esther's choice did not end up costing her life. But others have been less fortunate. Martin Luther King, Jr., made the choice to serve his people, to free them from the bondage of racism, bigotry, and indignity. It was profoundly the right choice, but it cost him his life. Yet it was in his dying that his message was made crystal clear, and his truth, merged with the great truths of the ages, calls us still to this very day.

Real choices are a spiritual wrestling match. They are a refusal to give in to the false illusions of power, wealth, security, and influence. Life-giving choices are almost always personally costly, professionally unwise, and finally, in the dark of night, richly rewarding.

We live in a world that is hungry, hurting, and so weary of war; a world fragmented and brokenhearted, yet yearning to be free and whole. It is a world that calls to us to make the choices that are life-giving. One thing is certain: each of us will have choices set before us that define our lives. But because all creation forms an intricate web, our choices are never ours alone. They are part of the fabric of life, and they are woven from many strands and many choices. Like Esther, we have come to the kingdom for just such a time as this. Our choices have cosmic significance. Our choices may not be as dramatic as Esther's, or as visceral as appearing before a dictator as bombs rain on his city, but there comes to us all in our lifetimes a choice that has that kind of character.

All choices that matter are ultimately choices of life and death. I cannot tell you what choices to make, nor can I see into a crystal ball that would tell us the results of the choices we make. But I can tell you that the faithful choice is always and forever to choose abundant life, full and free.

Not everyone can be an Esther or a Patriarch Pavle. But each of us can have a vision that sees the unity of all things, that comprehends deeply in our heart the power of love and is open, always, to reconciliation. When we do, we can say to ourselves, as Robert Frost wrote:

Two roads diverged in a wood, and I—
I took the one less traveled by,
And that has made all the difference.[2]

REFLECT

Thinking back over your own life, what choices would you define as life-changing? What did you decide? How did it make a difference?

PRAY

Lord, make me an instrument of your peace.
Where there is hatred, let me sow love;
where there is injury, pardon;
where there is doubt, faith;
where there is despair, hope;
where there is darkness, light;
and where there is sadness, joy.

O Divine Master, grant that I may not so much seek
to be consoled as to console;
to be understood as to understand;
to be loved as to love.
For it is in giving that we receive;
it is in pardoning that we are pardoned;
and it is in dying that we are born to eternal life.
Amen.

—ATTRIBUTED TO ST. FRANCIS OF ASSISI

The Beloved Community

There is one body and one Spirit, just as you were called to the one hope of your calling, one Lord, one faith, one baptism, one God and Father of all, who is above all and through all and in all.
—EPHESIANS 4:4–6

In the early years of Christianity, communities of believers gathered around the disciples who had walked with Jesus. Each community had its own unique way of understanding Jesus's message and living it out faithfully in their lives. As they spread all over the ancient Mediterranean world, some of these groups, as time went by, even produced their own written accounts—their Gospels—of the life and teachings of Jesus.

The community that grew up around the apostle John pictured a Jesus who lovingly washed the feet of his friends and commanded them to "love one another as I have loved you" (John 15:12). For this group of early Christians, living in the midst of the cruel and oppressive Roman Empire, love was the prime directive, and they became known as the "beloved community."

Nearly two millennia later, the Roman Empire is long gone but cruelty and oppression linger. In the 1960s, Martin Luther King, Jr., gathered a community around him that looked to the Gospel of John for inspiration as they sought to speak the truth in love. In the midst of a vibrant civil rights movement, he dared to push a nervous nation to see that economic rights and the end of poverty were necessary components of human rights. Pointing out this painful truth marked King for a martyr's death. But he left the world with his own prophetic vision of the Beloved Community.

King's enemies were desperate to silence his prophetic word and still the marching feet of those who worked with him in the civil rights movement. Those of us who believed in King and who had been transformed by his message wanted him to deal harshly with the enemy. They were, we told Dr. King time and again, dangerous. But his response would always be the same: his eyes would cloud up, and he would crease his brow and say that harsh treatment is not the way to deal with those who are dangerous, that "violence multiplies violence,"[1] and that "the strong person is the person who can cut off the chain of hate, the chain of evil."[2]

This was King's most persistent message, and the most difficult one for us to hear. "Time is cluttered with the wreckage of communities which surrendered to hatred and violence," he said. "For the salvation of our nation and the salvation of humankind, we must follow another way.... This is the only way to create the beloved community."[3]

The Beloved Community King believed in is not a gated, all-white, all-American, middle-class suburb. It is a community open to everyone who is willing to risk an encounter with the other.

The Beloved Community is not a place that is free of conflict, but a place where conflict is resolved nonviolently, where sins are confessed, where truth is told, where forgiveness is a concrete daily reality.

The Beloved Community is a sign that we are all God's children—each human is a unique, special, and precious creation of the almighty. The Beloved Community is a sign that our DNA is God's stamp, by love specially created. It is a sign that we are family, each responsible for the safety of all. That we are, after all, friends.

One of the most powerful images of the Beloved Community was in the World Trade Center the day the towers were felled. The Reverend Jon Walton, pastor of First Presbyterian Church, New York City, told me this story about a pastor of a Presbyterian church near the World Trade Center. The pastor, who buried thirty-five parishioners, tells the story of a survivor who said that the prayers lifted up that day by those who died and those who survived were said in seventy languages. Those prayers were prayed to a God of every name, faith, and nation. In their sorrow, in their dying, in their desperation and their hope, the people of God were one.

Even in the disaster of September 11, there were signs of hope. St. Paul's Chapel had been a place for quiet prayer—a museum preserved carefully and lovingly by the good people of the congregation of Trinity Church, Wall Street. It was, after all, the church where George Washington worshiped—his pew is proudly marked and painstakingly cared for. The back door of the chapel faced the gaping wound that is now a burial site for thousands.

As the events of September 11 unfolded, and as firemen and policemen, doctors, pastors, and politicians wearied themselves in a thousand acts of kindness, the clergy and staff of St. Paul's decided to open the doors of the little chapel to the rescue workers as a place for renewal of body and soul. Rather than a museum, that church became a living, breathing witness to love, to hope. Every pew became a bed, complete with quilt and pillow. George Washington's pew became a station staffed with volunteer doctors who ministered to the aching feet of the rescue workers. There was soothing music, and food cooked by some of New York's finest restaurants—the day I was there, the chef of the Waldorf Astoria provided the meal—was joyously and gratefully consumed.

The vestry worried about insurance liability, but the good people of St. Paul's just smiled. They knew in their hearts that what they were doing was right—maybe even righteous. The clergy in their rumpled garb glowed in their tiredness; in the midst of the death and destruction, life and hope emerged. You could almost hear the Lord of history saying, "If you love me, feed my sheep."

I am reminded of other ancient words written to a troubled people living in a troubled world. They too were wrestling with the meaning of the words of faith in a time not unlike our own, in which the qualities of love, patience, humility, and gentleness seem, in the words of Czech dissident leader Václav Havel, "like long-lost wanderers from a faraway time."[4] These words, written to the fledgling Christian community in the city of Ephesus, in what is now Turkey, were a clarion call to unity:

> There is one body and one Spirit, just as you were called to the one hope of your calling, one Lord, one faith, one baptism, one God and Father of all, who is above all and through all and in all.
> —EPHESIANS 4:4–6

These words continue to call us to unity today, despite war and terrorism, despite the rhetoric of the "axis of evil" and the multinational coalition waging war in Iraq and Afghanistan—despite everything—we are one people. War, poverty, and bigotry divide us and stand in stark contrast to this clarion call. Our challenge is this: Can we who have life and health and breath act as the one people we are called and created to be? Must it be that only in our dying we see the vision of our common humanity? Only in our remembrance that we pull together? Can we hope to be the Beloved Community—the one community—that Jesus called us to be, that Martin Luther King, Jr., reminded us to be?

September 11 was horrendous; it was a criminal assault on innocent people. It was unwarranted suffering, undeserved agony. But it joined us with all of God's children who have ever faced similar fates—those who have lived in slavery, those women and children who wander the world as refugees, those newborn babies who die because no medical help is available, and those who have lost loved ones at the hands of suicide bombers. They too make up the Beloved Community.

The United States might have come out of September 11 a stronger, less arrogant, more empathetic people. Our pain might have allowed us to identify with those who are hurting throughout the world. As the most powerful nation, we had the world's sympathy; everywhere, people shared our grief. The months and years after September 11 might have been a time of hope, not fear, a time when we could have allowed our undeserved suffering to pour out its redemptive blessing on our individual and national life. It might have been a time to nurture the Beloved Community.

But we did not make that choice. Rather we chose vengeance; we chose to show the world that those who took American lives would pay with their own lives. We turned our plowshares into swords and on the flimsiest of evidence, we broke with all tradition and leveled a preemptive strike against a people yearning for freedom from torture and oppression, and we wrought chaos. Our action turned the world's sympathy into puzzlement, sadness, disrespect, despair, and even hatred. The world expected more from us.

Instead, we became a nation filled with fear, obsessed with protecting ourselves from anyone who might hurt us. We failed to search for the source of the hatred of those who so horribly hurt us. And in our fear, we denied the hope that was the gift of our suffering. It is the suffering of the world that has given us models of hope that come from forgiveness and reconciliation. There are so many models we might have emulated.

There is the Parents Circle, formed by Palestinian and Israeli parents whose children have died at the hands of the other. Almost unbelievably, they have made a decision as parents to meet together and work on the process of reconciliation between their two peoples. They recognize the hurt, the anger, and the urge for retaliation, and yet they work with one another, insisting that unless they come together as parents, regardless of what happened to their children, other children will continue to suffer and die.

There is the family of Rabbi Irving and Blu Greenberg of New York City, whose son was killed in Israel. They did what he wanted them to do: at his request, all of his organs were donated to Palestinians.

There is the community of Neve Shalom, where families— Israelis and Palestinians—live together within the borders of Israel. Four hundred families are waiting to join that community. Even in the midst of turmoil there are signs of reconciliation and hope for the realization of a Beloved Community.

And there are the people I met on a trip to Cuba, a tiny island whose people suffer daily because of the United States' trade embargo that denies them much-needed food, medicine, and medical supplies. They could easily have resented our presence, even despised us, but they received us with grace and dignity.

At a government-run home for the elderly in Havana, some 150 residents between the ages of 85 and 108 lived in a building that was old and dark, with peeling paint everywhere you looked. If that facility were in the United States, we would close its doors. There were no paper goods, no adult diapers for the incontinent, not even a washer and dryer on the premises. Yet the staff served with joy, and the residents were busy, happy, satisfied. The air smelled sweet, with a palpable aura of caring.

The group I was visiting with wanted to help, and when we asked the staff what we could do, they did not ask for a washing machine or a year's supply of adult diapers. "What we could really use," they said, "are things to help entertain the residents and help them while away the time. Some videos, maybe, or some board games?" Their first thought was of making the residents happier—not making their own lives easier. They were hopeful people in the midst of a tragic and difficult situation. We came to bring help, but they taught us about hope.

People of faith are the harbingers of hope. It is we who must reclaim this nation, this world, for its highest purpose—liberty and justice for all. It is we who must breathe life into Lady Liberty with her outstretched arm prepared to embrace the world, her light of promise that dispels the darkness, beaconing the world's poor and oppressed to come to the place where there is hope—not just freedom, but hope.

The apostle Paul, writing to the Christian community in Rome, reminds them—and us—of the true meaning of hope:

> For in hope we were saved. Now hope that is seen is not hope. For who hopes for what is seen? But if we hope for what we do not see, we wait for it with patience.
> —ROMANS 8:24–25

Hope is our salvation today, too. This is a crucial time in America's history. Much is at stake. The world is waiting to see if this "Christian nation" can live beyond its fear, beyond its arrogance. Can we live into our hope? Can we rise up at home and abroad and be again God's people, freed from fear, ready to reclaim for our nation Isaiah's vision for the people of God where no child is born into calamity, where old people live out their days, where lion and lamb live together, where no one is hurt or destroyed on God's holy mountain? If we fail to participate energetically in choosing bold, brave leadership ready to seek peace and justice—not war, not vengeance—then whatever happens, we will bear our share of the responsibility.

We must gather up our bruised selves, for there are people to be fed, captives to be freed, lonely people to be loved, babies to be borne and nurtured. Hope is not cheap. It is not a solace for the sad or the disappointed, and it is surely not a reward for the victorious.

To be hopeful is our call, to bear witness in a doubtful world that the God of history has hold of us and we are not afraid to build the Beloved Community.

REFLECT

Has there been a time in your life when fear limited your choices? Were you able to overcome the fear? Can you identify today what makes you fearful? Are you able to move beyond the fear to a place of courage?

PRAY

God of justice and grace and mercy:
> You have always called your people to be future-pulled,
> not past-driven.
> You invite us to be co-creators in a world that is of your
> making.
> You urge us to risk—even to fail, looking toward a future
> that is beyond our knowing.

So with humility we pray for guidance as we risk setting forth our best ideas, in full recognition that your future will always be marked by your love for the whole of creation.

So with humility we pray for the courage to follow your will and your way, knowing that you care for every child created in your image.

We walk familiar grounds,

Are touched by the beauty of this familiar place,

Almost surprise ourselves as we quietly—
> with some embarrassment—

Declare our experiences spiritual.

So with humility we pray for a holy passion to claim minds and hearts as we move toward a future where success is measured by the finest in human values—a future of justice and mercy and love.

Finally, we are moved to pray for a kinder future for all who suffer, holding in our hearts all who face a future armed with faith alone.

We pray for ourselves, that we might never lose our urge to reach out beyond our own familiar borders.

So with gratitude and humility we receive the many gifts that have been entrusted to our safe keeping.

Teach us, Holy One, to share![5]

Part Three

Faith in Action

What good is it, my brothers and sisters, if you say you have
faith but do not have works? Can faith save you? If a brother or
sister is naked and lacks daily food, and if one of you says to
them, "Go in peace; keep warm and eat your fill," and yet you do
not supply their bodily needs, what is the good of that? So faith
by itself, if it has no works, is dead. But someone will say, "You
have faith and I have works." Show me your faith apart from
your works, and I by my works will show you my faith.

—JAMES 2:14–18

Catechisms and doctrines and learned theologians—they are all
well and good. But remember what Jesus was always telling his
apostles: Go. Get out there. Travel light and do what I'm doing. Faith
in action is a living, breathing faith that can change the world.

Here in part three, we will take a look at what it means to live our
faith in ordinary and not-so-ordinary circumstances.

The Road to Jerusalem

We often ask ourselves what the journey of faith is really about. We study the lives of saints and prophets, but our real question is, what about us ordinary people?

For generations Christians have sought guidance through studying the journey of Jesus. One thing becomes incandescently clear: God has claimed for us a high-risk adventure. For Jesus that adventure began in his own hometown and led finally to the cross and ultimately, we Christians believe, to the resurrection. So we become aware that the journey of faith is not for the fainthearted. Embarking on a spiritual journey means that life will never be well-ordered; rather, it will be interrupted when our plans are set aside for plans that are not of our making. If we come to say, "The Spirit of the Lord is upon me," be assured that path will open us to the surprises God has in store for us. We will discern the miraculous capacities of mind and heart.

Here are some guides for the journey:

1. Do not underrate the cost of the journey.
2. Begin at the beginning.
3. Claim the healing touch.
4. Break down the barriers that divide.
5. Forgive abundantly.
6. Take up your cross.
7. Be open to God's surprises.

I can assure you from my own life experiences that the journey of faith is exhilarating, exciting, and exhausting—and eventually it points the way to hope in a difficult and pain-filled world. Biblical references and stories open our eyes and our hearts to the journey of Jesus that provides guidance for us all. So let us begin.

DO NOT UNDERRATE THE COST OF THE JOURNEY

Outside the Palestinian city of Caesarea Philippi, Jesus prepared his disciples for the journey of faith. After describing the journey he gave them a stern warning "not to tell anyone that he was the Messiah" (Matthew 16:20). These words seem to be a strange contradiction to the message we have heard so often, "Go into all the world and proclaim the good news to the whole creation" (Mark 16:15). What was Jesus saying to his disciples—and also to us?

I imagine Jesus was saying that "you believe you know who I am, but the truth is yet to be revealed. If you live a life of faith, if you are to speak the truth, then you know there must be suffering."

> If any want to become my followers, let them deny themselves and take up their cross and follow me. For those who want to save their life will lose it, and those who lose their life for my sake will find it. For what will it profit them if they gain the whole world but forfeit their life? Or what will they give in return for their life?
> —MATTHEW 16:24–26

The words Jesus spoke were painful, and Jesus's disciples wanted to write a different story. Like all of us, they wanted the journey to be less uncertain. But Jesus was clear. If you choose the path of faith, the way will not be easy. But if you are willing to "lose your life" for his sake, then you will find it (Matthew 16:25).

Perhaps this is just the faith we need in these troubled times—a faith that is robust, life-claiming. And a faith that takes time and quietness to mature as God opens our questioning minds to truth. Consider, after all, the words attributed to St. Francis of Assisi: "Preach the gospel at all times; when necessary, use words."

BEGIN AT THE BEGINNING

Where does the journey of faith begin? At the beginning. To embrace our roots and start exactly where we are, we need to embark on the Christian journey from our hometown—which might be a geographical place or a state of mind.

For Jesus, it was both. Nazareth was the place where everybody knew him and his entire family, and the place from which he launched his ministry. He went to the synagogue, as he probably had done a thousand times before, chose the scroll of the prophet Isaiah, and stood up to read.

> The Spirit of the Lord is upon me,
> because he has anointed me
> to bring good news to the poor,
> He has sent me to proclaim release to the captives
> and recovery of sight to the blind,
> to let the oppressed go free,
> to proclaim the year of the Lord's favor.
> —LUKE 4:18–19

So far, so good. But before he sat back down, Jesus announced his mission. "Today," he proclaimed, "this scripture has been fulfilled in your hearing" (Luke 4:21). Jesus claimed for himself the role of prophet, acknowledging that God had called him to do God's own work. The Spirit was within him and he declared not in ordinary words, but in the words of the great prophet Isaiah, his life's passion. The hometown crowd, stunned, tried to throw him off a cliff. For Jesus—for us—doing God's work leads to trouble.

When, like Jesus, we claim our ministry, God's word becomes a living reality in our lives. Our goals and objectives aren't set forth by a management coach or a self-help guru. God makes a claim for our lives and changes them forever. Think, for example, of Moses: When he sees God in that burning bush he doesn't respond with his head: "Wow, I get it, I understand!" He questions his ability to respond to God's command. He claims inadequacy. He suggests his brother could take his place. But finally he responds with his heart, and with passionate action: "I must go to Pharaoh, I must free the captives, I must tell him to let my people go!" He does not ask the cost or the length of the journey or if his quest for freedom will be a success. He doesn't strategize about getting across the Red Sea. He knows exactly what the task is and accepts that God has claimed his life.

Jesus started out in Nazareth; Moses started out in Egypt. But the task remains for us to work toward. There are still the captives to be freed, the poor to receive the good news of generosity, the blind to be given sight, and all the world's oppressed to be blessed with justice.

God still calls each of us to this unfinished task. This is the future that God wills for all God's children: a future of peace, freedom, and dignity. We are not called to finish the task—how arrogant to think that if the battle for justice and dignity and freedom is not fulfilled in our time and by our hands, it is not worthwhile. We are but part of a long line of believers who have opened their hearts and hands to the Spirit of God. Together we walk toward the future God wills.

God has claimed us for God's purpose and that is a high-risk adventure that begins exactly where we are right now. If, like Jesus, we choose to say that the Spirit of God is upon us, the Spirit of God will open us up to opportunities we have never imagined and to discover the abilities of our minds and our hearts—beginning right where we are.

CLAIM THE HEALING TOUCH

Remember what Jesus said when he announced his call to ministry? Quoting from the prophet Isaiah, he announced that God had anointed him to bring "recovery of sight to the blind." It would not be possible to examine Jesus's teaching, his ethical and moral challenges to all generations—and to our own lives as followers of Jesus—without looking carefully at his healing ministry. The gospels are dominated by stories of healing that address human pain, weakness, and suffering. If you read with your heart, you will hear human cries for help in those stories of healing. The tears of suffering become apparent. Jesus sees it all.

In Mark 10:46–52, the gospel story of blind Bartimaeus, people looked at the suffering one who wanted access to Jesus as nothing more than an inconvenience and a bother. The gospel says that when Bartimaeus, who had been blind since birth, cried out, "Jesus, Son of David, have mercy on me!" (10:47), his neighbors in the crowd sternly ordered Bartimaeus to be quiet. Bartimaeus's suffering disrupted their well-ordered lives. But Jesus saw things differently. His sense of who mattered ordered his life and marked his ministry. It no doubt cost him his life, especially when he put healing above the law, to the ire of the religious establishment. What Jesus offered to the suffering one was not magic, but the miracle of his love, his care for the blind man, and his unbridled compassion that saw Bartimaeus as a brother.

Hear the power of Jesus's words: "Call him here." Those closest to Bartimaeus call to him, "Take heart; get up, he is calling you." And Jesus asks Bartimaeus, "What do you want me to do for you?" The blind man replies, "Rabbi, let me see again." Jesus responds, "Go; your faith has made you well" (10:49–52).

In one way the story is very unsatisfactory. We are told nothing of how the healing happened, offered no scientific explanation. All we know is that Jesus responded to the blind man's pain. Equally important, Bartimaeus, certain that Jesus could heal him, participated in his own healing. He believed and followed Jesus on his way. Like all of Jesus's healing stories, the meanings of the miracles are multiplied. Bartimaeus says to Jesus, "Let me see again." Was it more than just a case of physical sight, or was it a call for *insight*, a need to be renewed in faith? Is this part of the message, part of the miracle?

Here is a true story that offers deeper meaning to the simple story of Bartimaeus. It is a story about Andrew Young, my friend for many years. Andrew is a congregational minister, a man of deep faith. When he was mayor of Atlanta, he was deeply disturbed by the number of homeless people on the streets, and the city's apparent inability to address the issue. He told his staff that he wanted to better understand those who live on the streets, the roots of their problems, and the city's inadequate response. He was going to put on old clothes and be with the homeless for three days and two nights. His staff reacted a lot like Jesus's followers when Bartimaeus demanded his attention. "You're too busy," they said. "We need you in the office." Naysayers warned him, "Everyone knows you and you'll be recognized, so you'll learn nothing." But, as Mayor Young told me later, he was not dissuaded. He went. He walked, watched, talked, listened, learned. When he returned, his staff asked, "Well, what have you to teach us?" Young's reply was, "No one recognized me." No one looks into the faces of the poor.

How is that possible? As mayor of a major American city, Young was on the evening news; he was a frequent speaker at political events, civic meetings, churches. But this was different, he explained. No one looks into the faces of the homeless. There is no encounter. We simply do not see the person, only the problem. We are blind to their humanity. So it is with the hungry, the hurting, the hopeless, the jobless.

Like Jesus, we are called to look into the eyes of the Bartimaeus in our town, in our country, and ask what we can do to help. Our Christian task is to extend Jesus's healing hands to the world.

BREAK DOWN THE BARRIERS

For Christians of any stripe, unity is our call. We are called to be the one people God created us to be. Our origins, after all, are exactly the same. As the psalmist says, God has knit each of us together in our mother's womb (Psalm 139:13).

As always, Jesus is our model of unity. Think of the gospel: Jesus the prophet enters the stage and turns the religious world upside down, embracing love and challenging unjust laws. He calls us to be peacemakers, to be bold and brave in our search for justice. He heals the sick. He lives a life of mercy and forgiveness that reaches out to everyone, regardless of ethnicity, occupation, age, gender, or position on the socioeconomic ladder. He embraces the one people of God.

The night before his death, as his time on earth is measured in hours and minutes and marked with shattering disappointments, Jesus takes stock of his life and ministry. Facing certain death, he prays for all whom God loves—and that means every single human being (John 17:18–21). Jesus's embrace is wide and deep and inclusive. His reach touches all people. The signs are everywhere.

In speaking of Jesus's prayer of inclusiveness recorded in John's Gospel, one of our nation's finest African American preachers, the Reverend Dr. William Watley, pastor of the historic St. James African Methodist Episcopal Church in Newark, New Jersey, noted in a sermon in 2004 that we pray our most heartfelt prayers when facing death or disaster. Dr. Watley reminded us that it was when Jesus faced certain death that he chose to pray for our unity. Jesus prayed that we might be one so that the world might believe. Knowing our penchant for self-serving and destructive division, Jesus in his final prayer reminds us that we are all God's children and that our unity was the most fervent desire of his heart.

> I ask not only on behalf of these, but also on behalf of
> those who will believe in me through their word, that
> they may all be one. As you, Father, are in me and I am
> in you, may they also be in us, so that the world may
> believe that you have sent me. The glory that you have
> given me I have given them, so that you gave me, that
> they may be one, as we are one.
>
> —JOHN 17:20–22

This prayer has become, through the ages, the ecumenical, inter-faith prayer calling all people—Christians, Jews, Buddhists, Hindus, Muslims, nonbelievers—to tear down the walls of hatred, bigotry, and privilege, and to embrace one another in ministries of healing and justice-seeking. Make no mistake, this is not a prayer for Christians only, but for all humanity.

FORGIVE ABUNDANTLY

By the next day, the die was cast. Jesus was lifted to the cross. But Luke's Gospel reports a remarkable incident. Jesus, in his agony, turns to the thief on the cross beside him. He receives the thief's plea, his recognition of Jesus's divinity when he cries, "Jesus, remember me when you come into your kingdom." And Jesus, without asking any questions of the thief, recognizes him as a precious child of God. He insists on no spoken confession other than the obvious confession of his wrongdoing, and he says without hesitation, "Today you will be with me in Paradise" (Luke 23:42–43).

This is Jesus, our compassionate, grace-abounding, forgiving model. Out of the crucifixion—an experience of weakness, cowardice, agony, disappointment, pain, tears, rejection, and injustice—a thief was forgiven, hope was born. A faith was forged that continues to call us to lives of courage and forgiveness and compassion.

TAKE UP YOUR CROSS

After the suffering, the gospel offers a sign of hope, an act of courage. Joseph of Arimathea, a wealthy man, comes forward to claim Jesus's body, to provide a burial place for this man who died as a criminal. Risking his life, Joseph "takes up his own cross" and follows Jesus. He is an early witness to the courage of claiming the life of Jesus for our own.

The followers of Jesus have been witnesses to the miracle of his ministry, from the depths of human betrayal—their own included—to Jesus's undeserved suffering. Now they know what it means to claim Jesus, to take up the cross and follow his teaching.

Jesus is a very inconvenient human being. His teachings call us to a life lived not carefully or cautiously, but fully engaged with the world and with the messiness of humanity. Christianity is about *that* Jesus— the Jesus who fed the hungry, regardless of worth. *That* Jesus—who calls us to love our enemies and reminds us that it is easy to love those who love us back. *That* Jesus—who healed the sick even when it was against the law and marked him as dangerous to the people in charge. *That* Jesus calls us to take up the cross if we want to be his followers, insisting that those who want to save their lives will lose them, and those who lose their lives for the sake of the gospel will save them.

Most of all, Jesus calls us to a life beyond our own life, a life whose meaning is found beyond our own needs, our own possessions. Could this truth—this march to Jerusalem—be any more timely?

BE OPEN TO GOD'S SURPRISES

We cannot hide from the suffering of the world. We must enter into it. For it is in the struggle to alleviate suffering that we find our lives, freed from having to be God—that job is already taken. So on our own road to Jerusalem, we take up the cross of Jesus in the full knowledge that there in that act is the promise of resurrection and new life.

And that is the final guide—*be open to God's surprises*—as seen in the promise of resurrection and new life.

REFLECT

Think about the Jesus who is encountered in the gospel. What does his life say to you about the kind of life you would like to lead? Write down your own brief guidelines for your faith journey.

PRAY

God, you are a God of surprise.
Thank you, God, for the surprise of your love.
Open our hearts and minds to your truth.
  Amen.

Dangerous Dreams

*I am the good shepherd. I know my own and my own know
me, just as the Father knows me and I know the Father. And
I lay down my life for the sheep. I have other sheep that do
not belong to this fold. I must bring them also, and they will
listen to my voice. So there will be one flock, one shepherd.*

—JOHN 10:14–16

"The principle of compassion lies at the heart of all religious, ethical, and spiritual
traditions, calling us always to treat all others as we wish to be treated ourselves." With the reading of these words on November 9, 2009, best-
selling author Karen Armstrong unveiled the Charter for Compassion.
Drafting the charter took almost a year and, thanks to modern technology, now includes participants from around the world.

People of every faith, and those of no faith, publicly confessed,
in the words of the charter, that "we have failed to live compassionately and that some have even increased the sum of human misery in
the name of religion."

The Charter for Compassion welled up in Karen's heart and soul.
As she studied the world's religions, their differences were obvious, but
it was the common thread of compassion that ran through them all that
moved her. She was awarded the TED (Technology, Entertainment,
Design) Prize, which is given each year to an exceptional individual
with a vision to change the world. The award allowed Karen to fund

her deepest wish—her dream for the world—her dream of compassion, the hallmark of faith for every soul in every land.

In case this dream sounds simple, consider the words of the charter:

> Compassion impels us to work tirelessly to alleviate the suffering of our fellow creatures, to dethrone ourselves from the center of our world and put another there, and to honor the inviolable sanctity of every single human being, treating everybody, without exception, with absolute justice, equity and respect.

Listening to these words, in my bones I heard a familiar call to faithful action. I wanted to reach out, put my arms around Karen, and remind her that dreams can be dangerous, that any dream that takes faith seriously calls for nothing less than the willingness to risk—even to risk life itself. Back in the 1960s, Martin Luther King, Jr.'s, dream seemed clear and compelling, but it turned out to be very dangerous indeed. If you think that compassion is soft, that the familiar strains of *Kum Bah Yah* play quietly in the background, I invite you to think again. Our Christian heritage insists that we be open to all. The ethic of the Golden Rule belongs not just to us. The Golden Rule is a call to compassionate Christianity and if we take this call seriously we will need the courage born of faith. It is a call to a task that is difficult, messy, and fraught with risk. As we are reminded in the New Testament letter to the Hebrews, "Faith is the assurance of things hoped for, the conviction of things not seen" (Hebrews 11:1).

There are deep scriptural roots for a compassionate Christianity. It is a Christianity that takes seriously Jesus's most dangerous dream, that we might be *one*. In the seventeenth chapter of the Gospel of John, just before Jesus is crucified, his most passionate prayer is that his followers might live in unity, leading all the world to believe in his message.

The familiar story of the good shepherd lays the groundwork for the unity of all humankind and for the whole of creation. This story is one of my favorites. First, it paints a picture of a Jesus who loves his sheep and lays down his life for them. We who belong to his flock of Christians nestle into that comfort zone, for we are secure in and among our own. But as you may have noticed, Jesus never leaves us in our comfort zone. His truth always challenges us. There are others who do not belong to this flock but who know his voice and he will gather them also, and we will be one people.

In the story of the good shepherd, we encounter a Jesus not owned by Christians but who claims in his circle of care *all* God's children. This is a Jesus to be shared—not a parochial Jesus but an embracing Jesus, large and inclusive. It makes us squirm a little as our comfort zone is disrupted. There's only one flock, Jesus insists, so who is in and who is out?

There is no "ours" and "theirs" in the world of Jesus. There is no "other." The dream is that all are one. The story of the good shepherd is a challenge to Christian exclusivity and an affirmation of Christian civility and inclusivity. We are to hold all people as precious. I believe it is this understanding of faith that informed the thinking of Chautauqua founder John Heyl Vincent that we shall all bow at one common altar, the altar of love and compassion. He spoke words beyond our capacity to comprehend.

If we embrace the faiths of others, does this mean that we are to discard the faith of our ancestors, the faith that brought us this far? Not at all. Jesus tells us that if we believe in him, if our faith is rooted in his teachings, then we will reach out and embrace all of God's own. As Christians, we are called to an ecumenical, interfaith future rooted in our Christian faith. It is precisely because we are Christian that we accept the challenge that the scripture gives us to embrace the one flock of humanity.

All this could simply sound like good theology unless we root it in everyday life. Let me share a true story with you, told to me by a pastor friend of mine, whose church was very close to the World Trade Center. As you will see, it illumines the inclusive story of the good shepherd.

A young man in his twenties lived through the terror of being in the World Trade Center on the day the twin towers came down. He was on the forty-seventh floor and when the people were told to stay, his youth and his instincts told him otherwise. He ran down forty-seven flights to safety. So what was his problem? It wasn't survivor's guilt. It was this: he was unable to get out of his mind the scene that he left behind—people of all ages, races, genders, nationalities praying, in languages he could not understand, in postures of prayer with which he was unfamiliar. All were praying to one God.

He asked his pastor, "What am I to make of that? To whose God did they pray? Suddenly, my God seemed embarrassingly narrow." As he was running down the stairs, he couldn't help but think of the God who was claimed by all these people.

This young man had just encountered the one flock that Jesus calls us to. He had a vision of God's intent for humanity, a distinct expression of faith: one message, one God, one flock, one shepherd, one hope. He understood that God's intent for humanity is that we will be one people. In the midst of tragedy his life was completely changed. The hope for peace was perfectly clear. He had seen a vision, and his pastor helped him to see how it might direct his future.

Let us hope we might all glimpse such a future, for in that future is hope. Perhaps it is this vision that should be the passion of our hearts, a shared faith commitment that binds us together in a common struggle for a better world, a compassionate Christianity.

The United States is the most religiously diverse nation in the world. Thanks to the framers of the Constitution, no one religion is allowed to force its beliefs, however noble, on the body politic. People of every religion and of no religion are free to worship or not, as their conscience dictates. So perhaps we bear a special responsibility to create for the world a model of interfaith respect and cooperation.

That young man's question to his pastor was the right question. Who is this God we claim for ourselves? By whatever name we call God, God cannot be owned or contained within only one religion.

Does this mean that we are to be lukewarm about the faith of our childhood, whatever that may be? Quite the opposite. We are to be passionate believers, called to respect that same passion in the faith of others. Sounds easy, but it is not.

Does interfaith understanding matter in the grand scheme of things, or is it just a nice exercise for the religious in an increasingly secular society?

Today it matters enormously. Let me share an experience I had with Madeleine Albright when she was the secretary of state under President Bill Clinton. I served as a member of the U.S. Commission on International Religious Freedom. We stood steadfastly against exporting and imposing American Christianity to parts of the world that had their own treasured faiths and heritages. We discussed the need for diplomats and government leaders to understand the religions of our increasingly interconnected world. That was 1996; the governmental position was that religion was a private matter not necessary or helpful for diplomats or government leaders.

Then came September 11, 2001; and Madeleine Albright, like many, was deeply affected by those events. In *The Mighty and the Almighty: Reflections on America, God, and World Affairs*, Albright recognizes that culture and religion are yoked in much of the world. To be effective in the search for world peace required—demanded—an understanding of religion.[1]

Today, people of faith are newly valued and find themselves much in demand in the world of government. Here are just a few examples of how government and religion are connecting:

- The World Economic Forum now includes a faith community component.
- The Defense Department now has members of the faith community as part of their Western Hemisphere Institute for Security Cooperation.
- The U.S. Commission on International Religious Freedom is now a permanent feature of the federal government.
- Karen Armstrong regularly briefs members of Congress on the Islamic religion and on compassion, and quietly invites them to favor no one faith.
- Diana Eck, director of the Pluralism Project at Harvard University, was awarded the Presidential Medal of Honor for her groundbreaking work in honoring all religions, which is evidence of the government's respect for diversity.

Today, those in government recognize that understanding the diversity of religions is essential to building diplomatic relationships. President Barack Obama's speech in Cairo in June 2009 made this incandescently clear. Only at our peril can we ignore the importance of faith in shaping cultures and governments—in Iraq, Iran, China, India, Pakistan, Russia, Israel, and yes, Catholic Latin America and secular Europe. Compassion runs through all the world's religions and calls us to embrace this dream.

Instinctively that young man in the World Trade Center asked the right question. His amazement at their "one God" was spot on. Religious pluralism and interfaith understanding is no longer just living-room dialogue. It is a crucial component in the search for a peaceful world.

The world we are in—and the world of our children and grandchildren will be in—is increasingly an interfaith world. It will ask the very best from the religious faith that is in us; it will demand of us the living out of our finest values. It will require us to transform those terrible religious barriers into the bonds of our common, hopeful humanity. And from our religious variety, the faith we live by inside will touch our common life for the good of all.

This is the task the Charter for Compassion calls us to.

May God give us the vision, wisdom, and courage to be a compassionate people, and the imagination to bring about the New Jerusalem—a world of compassion and peace.

REFLECT

Read the Charter for Compassion that follows. Consider the part you and your community can play in making compassion a reality in our world.

THE CHARTER FOR COMPASSION

The principle of compassion lies at the heart of all religious, ethical, and spiritual traditions, calling us always to treat all others as we wish to be treated ourselves. Compassion impels us to work tirelessly to alleviate the suffering of our fellow creatures, to dethrone ourselves from the center of our world and put another there, and to honor the inviolable sanctity of every single human being, treating everybody, without exception, with absolute justice, equity, and respect.

It is also necessary in both public and private life to refrain consistently and empathically from inflicting pain. To act or speak violently out of spite, chauvinism, or self-interest, to impoverish, exploit or deny basic rights to anybody, and to incite hatred by denigrating others—even our enemies—is a denial of our common humanity. We acknowledge that we have failed to live compassionately and that some have even increased the sum of human misery in the name of religion.

We therefore call upon all men and women to restore compassion to the center of morality and religion; to return to the ancient principle that any interpretation of scripture that breeds violence, hatred or disdain is illegitimate; to ensure that youth are given accurate and respectful information about other traditions, religions and cultures; to encourage a positive appreciation of cultural and religious diversity; to cultivate an informed empathy with the suffering of all human beings— even those regarded as enemies.

We urgently need to make compassion a clear, luminous and dynamic force in our polarized world. Rooted in a principled determination to transcend selfishness, compassion can break down political, dogmatic, ideological and religious boundaries. Born of our deep interdependence, compassion is essential to human relationships and to a fulfilled humanity. It is the path to enlightenment, and indispensible to the creation of a just economy and a peaceful global community.[2]

PRAY

God, we are your people, holy and deeply loved. Help us to clothe ourselves with compassion, kindness, humility, gentleness, and patience. Give us the courage to bear with one another and to forgive one another, as you have forgiven us. Amen.

—BASED ON COLOSSIANS 3:12–13

Science and Religion

*The creation itself will be set free from its bondage to decay and
will obtain the freedom of the glory of the children of God.*
—ROMANS 8:21

T he people I have been privileged to know have changed me in
many ways, expanding my worldview, testing my faith, challenging my assumptions, and stretching my capacity to love. No one
fits this description more that Carl Sagan, an astronomer, author,
and self-proclaimed agnostic. Over the course of our friendship, we
talked together for hours about faith—what it was and why people
believed. Though we continued to disagree about the possibility of
God, we came to love and respect each other. Our conversations
bonded us in ways I cannot describe.

I met Carl in 1980, in the office of then Senator Al Gore. The
religious community was just beginning to grasp the environmental
challenge facing the world. Carl had returned from a historic meeting of Nobel laureates in Moscow. The scientists, along with a few
religious leaders, understood that our world was facing an unimagin-
able risk. But while the scientists' fears were based on fact, they
lacked the forum for turning that reality into a cause that might
change the thinking of large numbers of people. To address the
problem, Carl and his fellow scientists drafted an open letter to the
religious community, urging it to take up the cause of the environment as an issue of faith.

This letter led to the creation of what today is known as the National Religious Partnership for the Environment, which I have chaired for more than ten years. This organization is comprised of the U.S. Conference of Catholic Bishops, the Coalition on the Environment and Jewish Life, the Evangelical Environmental Network, and the thirty-six member churches of the National Council of the Churches of Christ in the USA (NCC). I was the general secretary of the NCC at the time of the partnership's creation.

The following is my response to their challenge, which first appeared in the book *Carl Sagan's Universe*.

■

Science and religion. Each one claims enormous human energy, power, and endless intellectual attention. Someone had a demonic sense of humor to allow me a mere few pages to discuss such an important subject. Nevertheless, the brevity is a blessing, for even in a longer paper no one could adequately address this topic. I have observed that virtually every contributor to this volume, including Carl and those who asked questions of him after his public lecture of the birthday symposium, have noted the existence of the world of religion.

Let me begin by trying to draw in the parameters of this large subject. The final section of this book has been designated "Science, Environment, and Public Policy," and I would like to focus on our communities—the community of science and the community of faith. Someone quipped that the evening party preceding Carl's birthday symposium was a collegium of graduate students several decades after; a class reunion; a warm, friendly, and vigorous community. In fact, the three of us in the small religious caucus [Dean James Morton of St. John the Divine in New York City, my colleague Dr. Albert Pennybacker, and myself] commented to one another that we were actually more comfortable in this gathering than we would be at a gathering of business leaders in the Chamber of Commerce. "Or," as the Dean said in a reflective moment, "perhaps in a gathering of church hierarchs." The communities of science and religion do not always or even often merit a favorable comparison. Throughout history our two communities have been seen as antagonists. Yet it is the possibility of a shared community that brings us together to address our present circumstances and our unfolding future.

This is not simply a matter of cutting the subject into manageable bites. It is that, but it is also recognition that old debates are essentially exhausted. To a large extent, old antipathies have been laid to rest, at least in the progressive religious community. Perhaps this has occurred for good reasons: a maturing of religious thought and a certain integrity, or even humility, in science's understanding of itself (which may be its sign of maturing). Antipathies also retreat in the context of realism about the major shift that has occurred. We now live in an age of science. At one time science struggled in an age of religion. Ours—the age of religion—was the ascendancy, and we did not handle it very well. We hope you will be more successful in this time of the ascendancy of science, and we will encourage that. (Dare we say we will pray for that, or was that what got us into trouble in our time?)

But beyond antipathy—out of the ancient, continuing place that religion holds and the ascendancy of science now comfortable with itself—there is the possibility of sharing our engagement with our common life and seeking a better way.

Let me tell you what I believe is an important story. It is a story of partnership, and it began with what Carl has described to me, at least apocryphally, as a direct, empirically verifiable, peer-reviewed experience of divine revelation! This somewhat secret story is about Dean James Morton's efforts to get the Episcopal Church to be more concerned about the environment. The Dean thought he had been successful when his church agreed to discuss stewardship nine years ago. Unfortunately, on the way to the convention they turned it into a discussion about funding, not about the environment. Determined to find a new strategy to capture church people's attention, he decided to issue a challenge to them from the scientists. Rather than choosing an encyclical, a movie, book, or television series, a letter was composed. It was titled "An Open Letter to the Religious Community," and history will mark it as a key, catalytic event that led to the permanent, irreversible integration of global environmental issues into mainstream American religious thought and life.

Few, perhaps no one but Carl, could have found the perfect refinement of tone that would communicate such authority, authenticity, and activism. Few could have identified and persuaded in just a few weeks thirty-two scientific colleagues of enormous stature to add their signatures. In the letter, the scientists said that humankind was close to committing (many would argue we are already committing) what in religious language would be called crimes against creation.

As much as you can encapsulate a breakthrough in a few words, the letter went on to say, "As scientists, many of us have had profound experiences of awe and reverence before the universe. We understand that what is regarded as sacred is more likely to be treated with care and respect. Our planetary home should be so regarded. Efforts to safeguard and cherish the environment need to be infused with a vision of the sacred." Lest you lose track here, these are the scientists speaking to the religious leaders.

That combination of urgency and deep recognition—across the distance and history that we share—of the dimension of the global crisis made the message strong and convincing. In a few more weeks, several hundred religious leaders cosigned a letter expressing immediate willingness to undertake earnest dialogue. The exchange of letters was formally announced at a meeting convened by President [Mikhail] Gorbachev in January 1990 at the height of perestroika. Such was the atmosphere of openness, hope, and possibility in which the letter was presented. Though I was not there, it is rumored that Gorbachev, and certainly [Minister of Foreign Affairs Eduard] Shevardnadze, joined in a chant invited by the Hindu priest in which all repeated the sacred word *om*. The story is told that later that night, and it was a Friday, a minyan of Jews celebrated Shabbat in a small room together for the first time within the walls of the Kremlin.

This letter led to two years of activity under a process known as the Joint Appeal by Religion and Science for the Environment, now called the Religious Partnership. Those discussions had many memorable moments. Once we were seeking to prepare another letter to present in the U.S. Capitol. The document was to be signed by Carl and the scientific community but also by representatives of the Southern Baptist Convention and others who are religiously conservative, not often a part of such ecumenical ventures. Some expressed concern about words that referred to global warming at a rate unprecedented in tens of millennia. "Some of us don't think we've been here that long," creationists said. Carl helped draft new words of consummate common sense: "We do not have to agree on [when or] how the natural world was made to be willing to work together to preserve it."

What does it take sometimes to set in motion significant movements of thought and action? One night, some years ago, one man, our friend Carl Sagan, decided that a letter needed to be written.

I believe that in our communities, in all our humanity, we are finding ways to address together the human predicament, the threat to this wondrous environment, and the diminishing of life as we know it. Good science and good religion are getting noticed! Bad science and bad religion have found it relatively easy to attract attention. For both it is usually rooted in self-service, dangerously so. Science can be socially naive, without ethical inquiry or restraint. Religion runs the risk of being unreflective, without integrity, or intent on lining its own coffers. It can become a theocratic movement that is neither harmless nor innocent. Imagine absolutist religion married to the power of our modern technology. It is a prospective but very possible nightmare. Our common life would become seriously threatened, and that matters. It is wrong and we all know it. It is up to the scientific community to say what is good science. I have no qualifications to speak about that. I can, however, speak about good religion, and it is good religion that needs to put bad religion in its place. Here I want to draw on the best of theological reflection, a field of disciplined, mature inquiry and thought about which many in the field of science cannot be expected to be broadly informed.

Good religion talks about ultimate, or primary, questions. When asked to define religion, Langdon Gilkey, a theological witness at the Little Rock, Arkansas, trial on creationism, suggests that religion holds to a certain view of the nature of reality; ultimate reality; reality as a whole. Further, religion centers its attention on the relationship of that ultimate reality to the deepest problems of men and women and even of nations: sin or alienation, finally from life itself; injustice; the abuse of life; death and rebirth. That is, religion addresses the question of the meaning of existence and it answers in terms of symbols, myths, teachings, scriptures, doctrines, and dogmas. When it is good religion, it answers in ways that resolve the deepest of human problems and build up the community of life.[1] Good religion does not build walls that divide.

Science is also a way of knowing reality. Perhaps it is our most reliable and fruitful way. Science is a wondrous power, engaging in proximate and largely immediate reality. It abstracts and objectifies and thereby equips us with the ability to understand and function in the midst of this setting for life that we have been given. Science helps answer the *how* maybe more than the *why* questions. Gilkey illustrates: "When it rains, we turn to the meteorologist to find out what caused the rain, and how it came into being and how it passes through. But when the bride asks, 'Why is it raining on my wedding day?' that is a religious question."[2]

Further, religion encourages a way of life steeped in renewal, redemption, and rebirth, which in turn provides the freedom to care, to risk, and to commit. That is, religion is found in lives that understand themselves related to God, the ultimate reality that religion affirms. In a way that parallels Carl's words in his paper, religion bat-

tles the "human conceit" and stands ready to dispute the philosoph-
ical claim that man is the measure of all things. Religion quotes the
psalmist in the scriptures: "What is man that thou art mindful of
him?" (Psalm 8).

Religion at its best leads to a sense of trust and a wondrous gratitude for the human capacities to share joy, to know love, and to live
in relationship to the ultimate reality that it affirms. "Amazing
grace," we sing, and in such dislodging of the human conceit, the
human capacity is truly freed.

Theologian H. Richard Niebuhr spoke of this way of life:

> Revelation is not something miraculously esoteric; it
> occurs in various spheres of human experience. Faith is
> not an irrational leap into the absurd: it is confidence
> and loyalty, aspects of common human experience.
> Moral life can be represented by the human activities of
> "makers," "citizens" and the "answerers," not only by the
> activities of moral philosophers. Ordinary human
> agents need no professional credentials to love and to
> care, and this is the way of life that matters.[3]

For Carl, for his wife, Annie, for me, and for those who have joined
in this partnership, this is the point of our coming together. This is
the way of life that Carl spoke of where we take stones from one
another's hands. I believe we are talking about the same vision. We
come with different words, different disciplines, real disagreements,
genuine respect, yet "the ground has been laid," as Martin Buber
would say, "for real and genuine dialogue." I believe that the ecumenical religious community can find a shared sense of life with the
scientific community. We can become partners.

Let me risk being teacher for a moment. When you read, "Religious
leaders say ... ," be advised that the media is not very interested in
moderate religious voices. Using your scientific skills, investigate such

claims rather than settling for stereotypes and prejudices. There are some religious voices and communities that are different, that are inclusive and ecumenical. These are the people who want to stop the book burnings and fight the religious control of public schools; who defend religious liberty because without it, there is no liberty at all. These are the folk who, with an eye for a sad history, insist on the separation of church and state, who oppose prayer in public schools, religiously regimented study, and every other officially privileged status for religion. And they oppose it on deeply religious grounds. When hundreds of HIV-positive Haitian refugees came to our shores, it was this community that settled every single one, in spite of our government's claim that the refugees should be sent back because no one would settle them. It is this community that has been jailed at the South African embassy, that presently risks the wrath of the religious right, that has ordained women and challenged patriarchy, and that awaits your scientific insights so that we might end our cruel homophobia.

What are some elements in our common ground? Already our experience with the Joint Appeal suggests several. Let me underscore three.

First, we share an emotion about the universe's beauty, mystery, and energy. We share a sense of wonder, respect, and affection for the world. Science has probed, assessed, and described with disciplined insight what the universe is in its unfolding. At no point is mature religion shattered or even compromised by such scientific insight. Our common ground is alluded to in Carl's 1985 novel *Contact*, when the person of faith says to the scientist: "You have made the universe large enough for the God in whom I believe." Ours is a common awe before the majesty of creation.

Second, science offers facts for men and women of faith. Religion has not been formed by the disciplined, evidential grasp of facts that science provides. For instance, a scientist here at Cornell wrote to me in anticipation of what I might say. In a thoughtful piece he called into question the way in which religious claims about the afterlife ignore the reality of bodily death. He pointed out the total absence of any credible evidence that anything in the human body survives. It made me recall the rhyme:

I had a dog; his name was Rover;
When he lived, he lived in clover;
When he died, he died all over.

Facts have to call religious claims to task and insist on their accountability. The question of the afterlife is a lecture all to itself and belongs to another occasion. The point is made, however. Religion and science have to deal with the facts that science provides with integrity.

Third, facts are critical. They are not morally and ethically neutral. Their accumulation, human knowledge, is not finally a bystander in life. Knowledge leads to power. This is also where religion and science meet. Once there is power, our question becomes one of ethics and morality: What shall we do with it? How shall we act? If religion is a realm of moral and ethical reflection, that reflection must also become a common ground for science and religion.

Out of these shared elements of our parallel life—emotional wonder, factual knowledge, and moral and ethical reflection—we can and must find a way to address together the conditions of life, which are often desperate.

Let me be practical. You have facts that are the product of disciplined thought and the hard work of investigation. We have a constituency of committed people who care. Suppose through ecumenical religious access, we mounted a program where every congregation welcomed to its pulpit a person of science to speak the facts urgently and passionately. Would that make a difference? What would it mean for the morally committed to be confronted with the facts and address what is happening to our world and our universe? Religion is pulled toward a livable future for all, just as much as it is driven by its tradition and its memory. Science is as well. A living partnership could be enriched and grow.

Does that sound too hopeful? Let's step aside and look at what has happened. Think of the image of planet Earth as a pale blue dot or, in its more familiar form, that wondrous sphere filled with blues, grays, and purples. Ponder its uncanny resemblance to the ultra-sound view of a mother's womb in the early stages of pregnancy. This image, a secular icon as it might be called in religious language, has helped form in our minds and hearts the reality of a world with-out walls; a world where barriers are broken and life breaks forth free and unfettered of the conceits of race, class, sexual preference, gen-der, and even nations.

Does it matter that the image of the world as womb hangs in a central place on the wall of the vice president's office? It is hard to know, impossible to prove, but something is happening. In less than a year, Palestinian leader Yasser Arafat and Israeli prime minister Yitzhak Rabin exchanged the handclasp of peace. Russian president Boris Yeltsin and U.S. president Bill Clinton stood together in the Rose Garden and talked of peace and cooperation. Nelson Mandela, thirty years a prisoner at the hands of the apartheid regime, took his place as the first black African president of South Africa, and four hundred years of white domination fell, an event every bit as signif-icant as the fall of the Berlin Wall. There is Ireland as well; and Jean-Bertrand Aristide boarded a U.S. plane and returned to power in Haiti. Old animosities are set aside, at least for the moment.

Who is to say what role the image of the pale blue dot played in these momentous events? Maybe none, but as for me and my house it makes a difference that science has given us the ability to see our tiny, insignificant world as a *tabula rasa* on which peace might replace the rivers of blood.[4]

REFLECT

Why should current environmental problems be a major priority for people of faith?

PRAY

Teach your children what we have taught our children, that the
  earth is our mother.
Whatever befalls the earth befalls the sons of the earth.
If men spit upon the ground, they spit upon themselves.
This we know: the earth does not belong to man—man
  belongs to the earth.
This we know.
All things are connected like the blood that unites one family.
All things are connected.

—CHIEF SEATTLE, 1854

On Prayer

Pray then in this way:
> Our Father in heaven,
> hallowed be your name.
> Your kingdom come.
> Your will be done,
> on earth as it is in heaven.
> Give us this day our daily bread.
> And forgive us our debts,
> as we also have forgiven our debtors.
> And do not bring us to the time of trial,
> but rescue us from the evil one.

For if you forgive others their trespasses, your heavenly
Father will also forgive you.

—MATTHEW 6:9–14

When I was growing up, my sister and I prayed together almost every night. Most often my father was the grown-up who joined us in our prayers, so he was the expert to whom our inevitable childhood questions about the benefits of prayer were addressed.

When I was about seven years old, a little girl in my class pestered me mercilessly. So I fervently prayed that she would mend her ways and be nicer to me. When her behavior didn't change—she was anything but nice—I told my father that I was done with praying. Either God wasn't listening, I figured, or God chose an answer I didn't like. My father wisely but not convincingly informed me that, as Jesus taught us in the Lord's Prayer, we always pray that *God's* will—not necessarily our own—be done. So what we ought to do when we pray, he explained, is to ask God for what we think is best for our lives, and God's response is just that. Only later did I learn that God's response to that childhood prayer taught me a lot of important lessons. It showed me to refuse to accept rejection, especially from a bully. It taught me to stand up for myself and it gave me strength. Much later, it taught me to have compassion for the life circumstances that created the bully in the first place.

But the most important lesson I learned, in a family that prayed almost every day, was that prayer is a way of talking to God. It is not an expectation of miracles, but rather a conversation that looks not for results but for life lessons. Prayer, at its best, is a source of strength and wisdom, listening to God's word and will for our lives.

In this book I have chosen a variety of prayers. None are my personal prayers. A few are prayers prayed with people facing painful, even life-ending, decisions. Most are what I call public prayers, those that speak in the context of worship or sometimes in a secular situation. As pastor to Chautauqua community, it is my privilege to discern the community's desires, and to pray in a way that challenges and gives words to their unspoken and shared concerns. For ten years I have prayed for Chautauqua's board of trustees. Some of their prayers are included in this book. Often, especially in the prayer below dated November 2008, the prayer gave words to their common anxieties, as the institution was facing budget dilemmas brought on by the economic crisis. Appropriately, that prayer offered the problem to God and asked simply that God's will be done.

I would like to look at three of the prayers I have offered in the course of my years of ministry. Maybe you will see something of your own experience in the situations and stories into which these prayers were woven.

A PRAYER OF HOPE

Founded in 1874, Chautauqua Institution has been a rich resource for lifelong learning, drawing over one hundred thousand visitors every summer to its historic site, where, in the course of its nine-week season, more than two thousand events are produced. The physical site and the program, encompassing the arts, education, religion, and recreation, combine to create a community whose entire purpose is engagement with ideas and between its participants. In this rich atmosphere, a dynamic interreligious environment has been developed and nurtured.

Since 2000, I have been honored to serve as the chair of the religion department at Chautauqua, where I work as pastor to the Chautauqua community, plan the religion lecture series, and officiate at the Sunday morning services.

A couple of years ago, Rindy Barmore, who serves as the executive assistant to Chautauqua's president, shared with me her concern for the health of her mother, Joanne. When it became clear that she was dying, Rindy's mom spoke with her pastor, who said that she must come to church and give her life to Jesus publicly. But her illness had made her too weak to leave the house, so she feared eternal punishment.

When I went to see her, responding to her faith crisis, she was physically weak but mentally strong, and very anxious about the punishment that she was told awaited her. I held her and listened to her confession of modest sins and told her she was forgiven, that God loved her—always had and always would. She sought assurance that I could only offer in my own limited human way. She was worried about letting go, yet the pain called her to peace. She worried about her children and her grandchildren—there was evidence of a loving life in her words. As we embraced, she asked me to write a prayer that she might read during her final days. This is that prayer, a prayer of hope that gave her peace and safe passage. Prayer can, I know from experience, bring hope even in a situation that might seem hopeless.

Great and Good God,

Your Son, Jesus, said, "Come unto me all who labor and are heavily burdened and I will give you rest."

Today I am weary and in so much pain. I have loved the life you so generously gave to me. I have fallen short of even my own expectations for goodness. I have tried, to the best of my ability, to be faithful. Forgive my failing—embrace my trying.

Now, O Lord, I am ready to lay my burdens down. Receive me into your loving arms. I feel the presence of your angels around me. They wait for me to be ready. Now I reach out my hands to you and pray that the saints will welcome me in peace.

I pray today for safe passage into an unknown tomorrow and I put my trust in Jesus.

Watch over my children and grandchildren. Love them as I do. Grant them a bright future.

Amen.[1]

A Blessing

The second prayer was given for Chautauqua's board of trustees in November 2008, soon after Barack Obama's election as the president of the United States. It was for many in America and throughout the world a victory over the racism that has plagued our country since the days of slavery, as the dream of liberty and justice for all lived in the shadow of the reality of inequality. Just prior to the board meeting, we faced the reality of the effect that the worldwide economic crisis would have on the institution's income and budget.

The prayer that follows speaks to a time of common concern and a shared yearning for a world free of violence. Of all the prayers to write, the most difficult are public prayers in secular settings. These require wrestling with everyone's God and internalizing our shared belief in the One who knows what we cannot know, yet has a concern for our human predicament. No wonder there are disbelievers! This is a love too full for us to grasp, so once again we pray in hope.

> God of Grace and Mercy,
> In the midst of turbulent and mercurial times, we dare to pray!
> We bow before you, the One whose love is from everlasting to everlasting,
> And whose gift to each and all is life—abundant, full, and free.
>
> Whether the market is up or down,
> Whether our candidate won or lost,
> We are reminded that, in God's world, we are one people,
> Called to a future in which peace is possible, poverty challenged,
> Prejudice unacceptable, and hope the constant companion of faith-filled people.
>
> In a hungry, hurting, and war-weary world,
> We pause to pray for our nation,
> Whose gateway remains guarded by Lady Liberty,
> Whose welcome is to the whole world,
> Whose torch carries the light of liberty and compassion.
>
> So in the sunshine of a historic election,
> And in the face of the grim reality of an economic tsunami, we pray:
>
> O God of Eternity, for whom a thousand years is but a day,
> We are grateful for this brief moment of borrowed time
> In which we live out our lives.

For this moment in history, given to us and to no other,
We ask for grace and wisdom and courage
That we might fashion from the clay of creation
A spirit of generosity.

So, God of Mercy, we lift up our new leaders.
We pray that you will raise up in them a passion for the
    good,
So that the values of many may translate into justice
    for all.

Surround these, your servants, with vision and passion
For a world made new and whole.

So we place our times, our nation, our world, and all who
    lead in your hands,
But we hold out our hands as well,
For in the end, God of Eternity, we all belong to you
And live in service to your will and to your way.[2]

MORNING PRAYERS

The third prayer is one that has been personally important to me in my ministry. I am deep in my roots an American. I am the descendant of families that came on the Mayflower; one of my ancestors, James Wilson, was a signer of the Declaration of Independence. My great-great-grandmother's house in Salineville, Ohio, was a stop on the Underground Railroad. My family's history is rich, striped with both patriotism and dissent.

I am the daughter of this family, a daughter of the American dream. I've been proud of that dream, and pained by our failure to live up to it. I am sure that my work in the civil rights movement, the peace movement, the women's movement, and the anti-apartheid movement are rooted both in a deep faith and a belief that we can be better people than we are. My years at the World Council of Churches exposed me to other nations' concentration on America's every flaw. At the same time, my eyes were opened to visions of peace and justice in nations oceans apart. So, honoring the flaws and gifts of every nation, how do we pray?

This prayer was offered at Chautauqua's ecumenical service of worship over several years when Sunday occurred on or just before Independence Day. And each time it has been prayed, some thirty-five hundred people have been in attendance, each searching for a way to honor our American dreams, confess our sins, and set forth hopes for the future. The prayer that follows is based on the hymn "America the Beautiful," written by Katharine Lee Bates in 1893. In it, we ask God to forgive our failures and stir in us the courage and compassion for a better nation within a cosmos created by a love beyond our capacity to imagine.

There will be four petitions, following the singing of "America the Beautiful."

> *America! America!*
> *God shed His grace on thee,*
> *and crown thy good with brotherhood*
> *from sea to shining sea.*

O God, you who come to us in our greatest joys and in our crushing sorrows, we come before your throne of grace and in full knowledge of and with grateful thanks for your healing power. We bring all who suffer, all who grieve, all for whom life has been an indescribable heartbreak.

Your love makes us bold to pray for ourselves as well as for others.

This week as we prepare for this nation's birthday, we remember all who are touched by our country's

power, by our vision, and by our decisions. We pray for
these United States on this birthday. We are a nation
blessed with waves of grain, majestic mountains, and
fruited plains. We give thanks for your great gifts and
pray for generous hearts that we might respond with
compassion to a hungry, hurting, war-weary world.

America! America!
God shed His grace on thee,
and crown thy good with brotherhood
from sea to shining sea.

Holy God: You created us for freedom. You called us out
of slavery, out of darkness into your miraculous light.
You sent among us pilgrims, prophets, peacemakers, who
dared to dream of an America that would be to the world
a sign and symbol of life, liberty, and justice for all. We
yearn for that America. Walk beside us, whisper that
vision of hope in our ear again and again until America's
flaws are perfected and liberty is laced with love and we
claim the whole world as our neighbor.

America! America!
God mend thine every flaw,
Confirm thy soul in self-control,
Thy liberty in law.

Merciful God: We give thanks for all who have gone
before us, for all who have and who continue to protect
our freedom, for all who gave their full measure of devotion—presidents, poets, teachers, preachers, soldiers,
pacifists, reformers, and conscientious objectors. In this
week of our national holiday, we pray for strength and

courage in our quest for peace. Remind us that the heart for peace stirs in every nation and in all people everywhere. Freedom is your gift to all your children. It is a gift in which we rejoice. May we tend it tenderly. It is ours to share, not ours to impose on others.

America! America!
May God thy gold refine,
'Til all success be nobleness
and every gain divine.

God of vision, who walks with us into the future: We pray for our alabaster cities stained with human tears. We pray for the day when misery will know relief, when war and bigotry are no more and mercy will mark all our dealings with one another. We pray today for the world's cities, their people, and their leaders.

God of the ages, mold us as a loving people, as people who live with extravagant love. Mold us into a healing nation inspired by the outreached hand of Lady Liberty, whose tear-stained face still dares to dream of an America where peace is possible, freedom is shared, and extravagant love will be the last word.

America! America!
God shed His grace on thee,
and crown thy good with brotherhood
from sea to shining sea.
Amen. [3]

■

Do I pray? Yes. I pray often—sometimes intentionally, and sometimes it just happens. I feel like I am talking to God, confessing all that I have not done or been. I pray for those I love and for those nobody loves. Music often opens me to prayer, freeing me from daily worries and helping me to find that place where prayer is possible. Prayer for me is akin to contemplation. It is a process that takes me outside of the trivial and opens me to a world beyond the dailiness of life. I expect no miracles and yet I entertain the possibility that there just might be one out there beyond my seeing or my doing.

My hope is rooted in my prayers. I do believe there is power beyond our imagining, and without question prayer sustains me in times of trouble and quiets my anxiety when situations seem to be more than can easily be understood or fixed. There is no proof that God exists, but I am strangely certain that prayers are heard and hope eternal is among us.

DISCUSSION GUIDE

Jenifer Gamber and Mariclair Partee

INTRODUCTION TO THE DISCUSSION GUIDE

Scripture references related to the chapter: The references to scripture included here are those cited as well as those embedded in the language of the author. Your group might choose one or two to read together using the process of *lectio divina* or joint reading and discussion.

Discussion questions: These questions are meant as starting points for conversation. Consider asking each member to prepare a response to one question before the group meets.

A guide for prayer: In his book *Engaging the Powers: Discernment and Resistance in a World of Domination,* Walter Wink asserts, "Social action without prayer is soulless; but prayer without action lacks integrity." The guide for prayer includes opening and closing prayers, and a reading from the Bible followed by questions for reflection.

Activities: Interactive exercises that provide additional ways to evaluate how our understanding of the chapter's themes might affect our lives and actions.

Final thoughts: Final thoughts suggest a conclusion to group study by asking, what are the implications of your discussion for your ministry in the world?

Love Matters

THEME: BONDS OF LOVE

In this chapter Joan Brown Campbell discusses the difficult task of determining which home, among multiple countries and family members and levels of relation, is the right one for little Elián González. Like Ruth and the Israelites, and Jesus after them, she ultimately comes to believe that home is defined not geographically, but by bonds of love.

In Deuteronomy 26:5, the descendants of Abraham are instructed to profess their genealogies before the altar of the Lord as they make their sacrifices in the temple: "My father was a wandering Aramean, and he went down into Egypt with a few people and lived there and became a great nation, powerful and numerous." In this way the Lord knows who they are, the bonds that they share, and where they call home. Home is of utmost importance in the Hebrew Bible, and to the people to whom these scriptures were originally addressed. If one knew where strangers called home, one could determine all sorts of facts about them—what tribe they belonged to, what family they came from, what gods they worshiped— and they would no longer be strangers.

The world of the Hebrew scriptures was diverse. Many different peoples lived side by side, traded with each other, and worshiped many gods. Often followers of one god would also make sacrifices to the gods of their neighbors and business associates, or, as they traveled, to the gods of foreign lands. In the divine realm, they covered all their bases. The God of Abraham was unique in his demand that his followers forsake all other gods. Prohibitions against graven images and idols and stories of the perils of turning to other gods (such as the golden calf) fill the Hebrew scriptures and act as cautionary tales to those who have pledged themselves to the God of Israel. In exchange for forsaking other gods and following the laws laid out for them, God promised Abraham and his descendants a "homeland" and a heavenly country (Genesis 12:1–3, quoted in Hebrews 11:12–16).

In becoming the people of God, the Israelites entered a new sort of citizenship, and renounced the physical places of their birth for the heavenly home of their God's love. Renouncing the protection of home was no small gesture. In an often cruel and lawless world, it meant turning one's back on the only place that assured safety and refuge. This is what makes Ruth such a radical character when she refuses to return to the home of her mother after her husband's death (Ruth 1:8–17). By choosing to remain with her mother-in-law, Naomi, Ruth willingly abandons the protection of her ancestral home and its gods, and commits to the sole protection of an unknown God of a foreign land and foreign people. She also willingly risks her virtue, and thus her position in society, to become a woman without the protection of a father or other male relative. Homeless women without protection were at great risk of sexual abuse or assault, and much like the scores of women and children trafficked internationally today as sexual slaves, they suffered silently in a society that, if not complicit in, was blind to their plight.

Ruth redefines home, exchanging the solidness of geography for the bonds of love and community. Jesus similarly instructs his disciples in regard to earthly bonds of family and home: "I have come to set a man against his father, and a daughter against her mother, and a daughter-in-law against her mother-in-law.... Whoever loves father or mother more than me is not worthy of me; and whoever loves son or daughter more than me is not worthy of me; and whoever does not take up the cross and follow me is not worthy of me" (Matthew 10:35–38). Jesus redefines home no longer by bonds of family, but by bonds of communal love.

For Elián González, the question of home became embroiled with politics. Elián's well-being became a secondary concern. Leaders of the U.S. faith community joined Reverend Dr. Joan Brown Campbell and the National Council of Churches in defining home and family as that place where love resides. People of faith, as in days of old, define home not by comfort and plenty but by love.

SCRIPTURE REFERENCES RELATED TO THE CHAPTER
Matthew 2:13–23
Matthew 19:13–15
1 Corinthians 13:13
Colossians 3:14–15

DISCUSSION QUESTIONS

1. The resolution to return Elián to his family in Cuba was ultimately decided by the United States Supreme Court based on a tricky legal question: can a person legally petition for asylum for a relative who is not a direct descendant? But the court's decision perhaps raised a more important question: what place does love have—or should it have—in the legal system?

2. How might the author's suggestion that *love* makes a family inform debate about legislation that affects LGBTQ families?

3. An upsurge in deportations of undocumented immigrants from the United States to their home countries is breaking nuclear families apart. What place does the bond of love have—or should it have—in determining U.S. immigration policy? In the deportation of undocumented immigrants?

4. Juan Miguel González, Elián's father, took a leap of faith in coming to the United States to bring his son home. What leap of faith have you taken in the name of justice, knowing that your actions might not be effective? What sustained you during the time of uncertainty?

5. In 2009, average per capita income was just under $10,000 in Cuba, compared to more than $40,000 in the United States. Children growing up in the United States arguably have more economic opportunities than in Cuba. However, all Cuban citizens are guaranteed an education, free medical care, and food on their table. What role should these differences have played in deciding whether Elián should be returned to his family in Cuba?

A GUIDE FOR PRAYER

1. Opening prayer

Holy God, comforter and judge; as Mary wept for her son and Rachel wept for her children, let us never cease to cry out on behalf of all children who suffer at the hands of power and injustice. Mercifully grant that we, walking in your way, do not cause more suffering to one another and the creation but find the paths of true justice and righteousness. Amen.[1]

2. Scripture reading

While he was still speaking to the crowds, his mother and his brothers were standing outside, wanting to speak to him. Someone told him, "Look, your mother and your brothers are standing outside, wanting to speak to you." But to the one who had told him this, Jesus replied, "Who is my mother, and who are my brothers?" And pointing to his disciples, he said, "Here are my mother and my brothers! For whoever does the will of my Father in heaven is my brother and sister and mother."

—MATTHEW 12:46–50

3. Questions for reflection

How does Jesus define family?

How does his definition challenge or affirm how today's culture defines family?

How does the definition of family affect your decisions?

4. Closing prayer

God of Compassion, source of faith, hope and love, teach us to honor those who need our help, that we may give without condescension, and receive with humility. Show us how to give you what we have, for nothing is too big or small for us to offer, or for you to use. Amen.[2]

ACTIVITY

Ask all members of the group to write their first and last names on a large piece of paper for the whole group to see. Have each person explain the history and meaning of their names. After everyone has contributed, ask the group how their names contribute to their sense of identity and "home."

FINAL THOUGHTS

Based on the chapter and your exploration of it, what causes you sorrow? What inspires hope? What action might you take to address each?

Bearing Down in Love

THEME: UNITY IN DIVERSITY

Campbell begins this chapter by examining the institution of slavery in the United States, and the impact, almost 150 years after slavery was legally abolished, it has had on Americans of all races. Campbell praises the virtue of unity amid diversity by pointing to New York City, which celebrates the many nationalities, races, and creeds that not only exist but thrive in its streets and neighborhoods. Campbell notes that this fierce unity allowed New Yorkers to band together after the tragedy of September 11, 2001. Today, a revitalized New York is a tribute to the power of the spirit and the value of many cultures coming together in one place, sharing one spirit.

Throughout the Christian scriptures, Jesus and his disciples talk of a heavenly city, a New Jerusalem, also referred to as the city or kingdom of God, or of heaven (Matthew 7:21; Mark 12:34; Luke 17:20–21; Revelation 3:12, 21:2). Building on the notion of kingdom set forth throughout the Hebrew scriptures as the fulfillment of the covenants that God made with Abraham and David, Jesus describes this heavenly city primarily through parables. The kingdom of God is described alternately as a seed sown in different qualities of soil, a field of wheat in which weeds have also grown, the growth cycle of a crop, a mustard seed, yeast within flour, and a treasure hidden in a field. All of these parables support the kingdom of heaven as something that starts very small, in the barest existence of faith, and grows into something large or very valuable, beyond the measure of its beginnings, as faith spreads and faithful people change the world.

Jesus instructs his followers to pray for the coming of this kingdom in the Lord's Prayer, asking that God's "kingdom come, [God's] will be done, on earth as it is in heaven" (Matthew 6:10). Biblical scholars and theologians have argued for generations about the nature of this New Jerusalem. Does it exist on the temporal plane or the spiritual? Will its coming mark the coming of the Messiah or does it already exist here and now, among all who live lives guided by faith? What is clear is that this heavenly city is one of unity and love, where all people will live in unity with God, where "mourning and crying and pain will be no more" (Revelation 21:4).

A modern retelling of this well-known scriptural passage, echoing Campbell's thoughts in this chapter, might describe a community where all people view each other as members of a family, unburdened by considerations of race, gender, class, or creed. It might describe a heaven on earth, where slavery, war, and other violations of humanity are remembered as cautionary artifacts of an unenlightened time and people. We are exhorted throughout the Bible and throughout history—particularly by our history's failures—to bear down, just like that mother bearing down in the birth process, and strive to make the kingdom of God present in our daily lives. And just like that mother, we will know that we have almost achieved our goal when we feel we cannot go on, cannot give any more of ourselves, cannot continue. Then we will know that we are truly sharing in divine work, and the kingdom of heaven is at hand.

SCRIPTURE REFERENCES RELATED TO THE CHAPTER
Exodus 34:6–7
Matthew 12:25
Matthew 12:46–50
John 10:7–21
Ephesians 4:1–7

DISCUSSION QUESTIONS
1. Name the types of diversity in your town or city. Other than geographic proximity, what unifies the people who live there?
2. What divisions are evident in your town or city? What impact do these divisions have on political decisions?
3. How inclusively do you draw the circle of your family? How do you express this definition of family?
4. The distribution of goods within a family likely follows a socialist paradigm—each is expected to contribute according to her ability, each

receives according to her needs. What obstacles does society face in distributing goods according to an expanded view of family, as suggested by the author?

5. Martin Luther King, Jr., calls love "the most durable power in the world." How have you seen love endure in your life? How does love call us to "bear with" our neighbors? How is this request reasonable? How is it unreasonable?

6. What does it mean to bear with one another? What risks are involved? What promises are needed?

A Guide for Prayer

1. Opening prayer

God, whose love breaks the barriers that divide, bind creation to your heart into one spirit, one hope and one desire that our being and our doing glorify you and all creation. Make your delight in creation our delight in serving one another.[3]

2. Scripture reading

The Lord works vindication
    and justice for all who are oppressed.
He made known his ways to Moses,
    his acts to the people of Israel.
The Lord is merciful and gracious,
    slow to anger and abounding in steadfast love.
He will not always accuse,
    nor will he keep his anger forever.
He does not deal with us according to our sins,
    nor repay us according to our iniquities.
For as the heavens are high above the earth,
    so great is his steadfast love toward those who fear him;
as far as the east is from the west,
    so far he removes our transgressions from us.
As a father has compassion for his children,
    so the Lord has compassion for those who fear him

for he knows how we were made;
he remembers that we are dust.
—PSALM 103:6–14

3. Questions for reflection

How would you characterize God's love in this psalm?
How does this love suggest that the members of God's family
are bound into one?

4. Closing prayer

Set me as a seal upon your heart,
as a seal upon your arm;
for love is strong as death,
passion fierce as the grave.
Its flashes are flashes of fire,
a raging flame.
Many waters cannot quench love,
neither can floods drown it.
If one offered for love
all the wealth of one's house,
it would be utterly scorned.
—SONG OF SOLOMON 8:6–7

ACTIVITY

Go to www.un.org/millenniumgoals to answer and discuss the following
questions:

- What are the eight Millennium Development Goals?
- Are there goals that you believe are missing? If so, what are they?
- Which goals do you believe are most pressing?
- Which goal do you feel called to address in your life?

FINAL THOUGHTS

Based on the chapter and your exploration of it, what causes you sorrow?
What inspires hope? What action might you take to address each?

Who Is My Neighbor?

THEME: NEIGHBORS

Who is my neighbor? This is the question Campbell ponders in this chapter, the same question asked of Jesus by a man well versed in the law in the Gospel of Luke (10:25–37). Jesus's reply reveals the heart of Christianity.

The story of the good Samaritan is woven into the fabric of our lives. On its face it is a story of the sin of artificial divisions getting in the way of shared humanity, as travelers—a priest, a Levite, all good and faithful people—passed by a wounded man in the gutter. It was only a Samaritan—hated and reviled, untouchable—who stopped and gave aid. The sin of not helping is made greater by the sin of hypocrisy: the priest and the Levite considered themselves men of God, yet would not help a man in need. When the Samaritan risked his own safety and spent his own resources to ensure the protection and care of the traveler, the Samaritan showed hatred for all sin. He despised the sin of the robbers who attacked the traveler, the sin of the "godly" men who failed to offer assistance, and the sin he himself had suffered at the hands of those who, because of his ethnicity, held him apart as somehow not quite human.

This parable is lived out too often in our daily lives. Citizens rally against undocumented immigrants, who are denied their humanity doing the jobs no Americans will do, who are disproportionately targets of crime, and who suffer contempt from those whose own relatives immigrated not so many generations ago. The parable is lived out when those who have the means to afford health insurance are given priority over those who cannot, and when our politicians rail against giving government "handouts" for the basic human right to health. Too often, our answer to the national debate of "Who is my neighbor?" is, "Those who look like me, earn like me, and think and vote like me." This ugly reality flies in the face of Jesus's response to the young man who questions him in Luke's story.

Campbell describes this sin as "the human conceit," a self-centered-ness in the most literal sense, a belief that we are entitled to special privileges because of our race, station in life, or class. Though it may seem that we are currently developing this willful disregard for others on a scale unknown to those who lived before us, the sin is not new. Thousands of years before Jesus told his story of the good Samaritan, the prophet Micah professed a similar truth: "What does the Lord require of you but to do justice and to love kindness, and to walk humbly with your God?" (Micah 6:8). Diversity working together in unity, Campbell says, is the basis for life. It is also the basis for a faithful, well-lived life. Good religion, Campbell notes, encourages a way of life steeped in renewal, redemption, and rebirth, which provide the freedom and courage to acknowledge a stranger or an enemy as a neighbor. Justice, compassion, and humility: these three things are required of us by God, and yet we continually struggle to see the face of God in those for whom we feel contempt or disgust. If we can free ourselves from our own cynicism, our own protective instincts, we can live in the light of God for all of our days.

SCRIPTURE REFERENCES RELATED TO THE CHAPTER
Psalm 8:4
Micah 6:8
Luke 10:25–37

DISCUSSION QUESTIONS
1. Who are the good Samaritans in your life or community? How are they outcasts? How do they help heal the broken?
2. Where are the clothes you are wearing right now made? What do you know about the conditions under which they were made? If this is a concern for you, how do you envision taking action?
3. Do you believe there is life on other planets? What are the implications of your answer to the choices you make?
4. What are ways that globalization is a positive force in our world? A negative force? How has globalization directly affected you?

5. What is a source of diversity in your life? How does it sustain and challenge the cohesiveness of the community?
6. What are words you use to describe God? How do they reflect who you are? How do these words limit or expand your sense of the Divine?

A GUIDE FOR PRAYER

1. Opening prayer

O God, in whom nothing can live but as it lives in love, grant us the spirit of love which does not want to be rewarded, honored or esteemed, but only to become the blessing and happiness of everything that wants it; love which is the very joy of life, and thine own goodness and truth within the soul; who thyself art love, and by love our redeemer, from eternity to eternity.[4]

2. Scripture reading

By the streams the birds of the air have their habitation;
>   they sing among the branches.
From your lofty abode you water the mountains;
>   the earth is satisfied with the fruit of your work.
You cause the grass to grow for the cattle,
>   and plants for people to use, to bring forth food from the
>   earth,
and wine to gladden the human heart,
>   oil to make the face shine, and bread to strengthen the
>   human heart.
The trees of the Lord are watered abundantly,
>   the cedars of Lebanon that he planted.
In them the birds build their nests;
>   the stork has its home in the fir trees.
The high mountains are for the wild goats;
>   the rocks are a refuge for the coneys.

You have made the moon to mark the seasons;
    the sun knows its time for setting.
You make darkness, and it is night,
    when all the animals of the forest come creeping out.
The young lions roar for their prey,
    seeking their food from God.
When the sun rises,
    they withdraw and lie down in their dens.
People go out to their work
    and to their labor until the evening.
                                —PSALM 104:12–23

3. Questions for reflection

Why do you suppose the psalmist wrote this psalm?
How is wonder for creation cultivated in our society today?
How might our society's sense of wonder be awakened?

4. Closing prayer

O God, you made us in your own image and redeemed us through Jesus your Son: Look with compassion on the whole human family; take away the arrogance and hatred which infect our hearts; break down the walls that separate us; unite us in bonds of love; and work through our struggle and confusion to accomplish your purposes on earth; that, in your good time, all nations and races may serve you in harmony around your heavenly throne; through Jesus our Lord. Amen.[5]

ACTIVITIES

1. Find a photograph of a spiderweb to look at together as a group and consider the metaphor of a web with these questions:
   - What is a web like?
   - What challenges does a web present?
   - What parts of your life can be characterized by a web?[6]

2. Pass out index cards and ask each person to write an answer to the question, who is my neighbor? After everyone is finished, share your answers and discuss the various answers. What impact might the answers have on the action each of you takes in your community?

FINAL THOUGHTS

Based on the chapter and your exploration of it, what causes you sorrow? What inspires hope? What action might you take to address each?

One Shepherd, One Flock

Theme: Beyond Boundaries

Relying on the parable of the good shepherd (John 10:1–21), Campbell speaks eloquently in this chapter about her understanding of a biblical mandate for ecumenical and interfaith work. She likens the various denominations and religious faiths to individual sheep within the fold. As sheep, our responsibility is to the shepherd; we must know his voice and follow him. It is the job of the shepherd to separate and divide those who belong in the flock and those who do not, but often we sheep forget our role. We try to pervert the order of things, to follow the voices of strangers. We may try to steal and destroy when instead we could have life; we may struggle unsuccessfully to wield the shepherd's staff our-selves. All the while, the truth—if we would only hear it—is free and easy.

In this parable, Jesus describes himself not only as the shepherd, but also as the gate. Those who would climb over him or skirt around him are thieves and bandits, attempting to take by force or trickery that which he offers in love. Those who enter through the gate of the love of God will have a life of peace.

Notice that Jesus does not limit his watch to a single sheep, or even a single flock, but to the multitudes that make up his fold, and who find safety and sustenance through God. Jesus reminds us, "I have other sheep that do not belong to this fold." Unlike one who is paid to watch over the sheep of others, Jesus tends to us with the devotion of a parent to a child. We are the people of his pasture, and the sheep of his hand, and he will stop at nothing to keep us safe.

Campbell sees in this description of the shepherd and his sheep a call to define ourselves as people of God, and to embrace others who root their identity in God as well, even if we differ in our understanding of who that God is. We live in a time of unprecedented religious plural-ism, and it is tempting to focus our energies on defining who is wrong and who is right, to limit the definition of neighbor. This is even more tempting as we see, around the globe, people committing great atrocities against one another in the name of God, however they define God.

Our fear can cause us to close the ranks against those sheep we do not recognize as our own, when instead we should listen always for the voice of our shepherd, which calls clearly to us to serve God in faith and charity for the good of humankind. It is safe to assume that those calling out messages of destruction or death are false shepherds. So we must strive to carry out God's mandate to love our neighbor without dividing and defining who is in and who is out of God's fold. It is not an easy task, and it seems that it is never accomplished. But Campbell reminds us that we do not hope for what we see before us, but for what we do not see. As we are told in the letter to the Hebrews, "Let us also lay aside every weight and the sin that clings so closely, and let us run with perseverance the race that is set before us" (Hebrews 12:1). As we run, let us have patience, until we hear the voice of our Good Shepherd, calling us home.

SCRIPTURE REFERENCES RELATED TO THE CHAPTER
John 10:11–18
2 Timothy 4:1–8
Revelation 21:1–4

DISCUSSION QUESTIONS
1. How can being rooted in your own faith open the way for inter-denominational and interfaith dialogue? Could grounding in your own faith be a barrier to dialogue?
2. What faith traditions are represented in your study group? What denominations? What denominations have members of your group belonged to in the past? What can you do to invite greater diversity?
3. Jesus said, "I have other sheep that do not belong to this fold. I must bring them also" (John 10:16). He also said, "I am the way, and the truth, and the life. No one comes to the Father except through me" (John 14:6). How do you reconcile these two verses?

4. The author says that we separate people by such things as race, gender, and class. Are there circumstances under which divisions could be helpful?

5. Cardinal Edward Idris Cassidy suggested climbing a mountain as a metaphor for the search for Christian unity. Which part of the climb are you currently on? What provisions have you made to help you endure the journey?

A GUIDE FOR PRAYER

1. Opening prayer (said as a call and response)

Across the barriers that divide race from race:
Reconcile us, O Christ, by your cross.

Across the barriers that divide rich from poor:
Reconcile us, O Christ, by your cross.

Across the barriers that divide people of different cultures:
Reconcile us, O Christ, by your cross.

Across the barriers that divide Christians:
Reconcile us, O Christ, by your cross.

Across the barriers that divide men and women, young and old:
Reconcile us, O Christ, by your cross.

Confront us, O Christ, with the hidden prejudices and fears
that deny and betray our prayers.
Enable us to see the causes of strife, remove from us all sense
of superiority.
Teach us to grow in unity with all God's children.[7]

2. Scripture reading

I therefore, the prisoner in the Lord, beg you to lead a life worthy of the calling to which you have been called, with all humility and gentleness, with patience, bearing with one another in love, making every effort to maintain the unity of the Spirit in the bond of peace. There is one body and one Spirit, just as you were called to the one hope of your calling, one Lord, one faith, one baptism, one God and Father of all, who is above all and through all and in all.

—EPHESIANS 4:1–6

3. Questions for reflection

How do you interpret the phrase "who is above all and through all and in all" in terms of Christian unity?
How does this verse challenge you?

4. Closing prayer

When we rejoice in the freedom that you give us, strengthen us with compassion for our sisters and brothers, the friend and the stranger, knowing that we are all nourished by the gift of your very self. Amen.[8]

ACTIVITY

Go to www.oikoumene.org/en/resources/videos.html and choose a video to watch and discuss as a group. Your group might also choose to plan a week of prayer for Christian unity in your place of worship.

FINAL THOUGHTS

Based on the chapter and your exploration of it, what causes you sorrow? What inspires hope? What action might you take to address each?

Sacred Conversation

THEME: THE COST OF DISCIPLESHIP

What does it cost to be a Christian? Only love of God, and love of neighbor (Matthew 22:36–40, Mark 12:30–31, Luke 10:27). But it may also cost you all that you hold dear—your standing in the community, your family, even your life. Campbell describes her development as a Christian during a time of struggle for civil rights for African Americans. Though she was already a mother and a wife, living a comfortable life full of privilege and power, she had a limited understanding of Christian faith, until its message hit home. As she worked for the equal rights of African American citizens in her community, she began to lose those things that she had once counted as most precious. Her marriage ended, her life of home and leisure became one devoted to work in the community, and she found that she was a new person, defined by the faith for which she had sacrificed. In return for a change in station, for the surrender of the privileges and power of an upper-middle-class wife, she received a life rich in experience, in hard work for justice and equality. And ultimately, as she watched her daughter become the first woman mayor of Cleveland, she received the gift of knowing that her work had inspired the generations to come after her.

Christian history is full of individuals who traded comfort and happiness for strife, ill-treatment, and sometimes death, all out of love of God. We call some of these men and women saints, others we call martyrs, but all were faithful believers, willing to make the ultimate sacrifice for Jesus. Many of the early Christians were cast out of home and society for their beliefs, abandoned by family and community, all because they chose to follow God. In 177 CE, St. Blandina, a slave girl, and her companions were gruesomely tortured by the Roman government in Lyons and torn apart by wild beasts, all because they were unwilling to deny God. After

Christianity was adopted by Constantine in the fourth century, these state-imposed martyrdoms became rare, but sacrifices continued.

Campbell tells the story of Beyers Naudé, a South African clergyman who lost considerable status because of his opposition to apartheid. In Germany during the reign of Hitler, many clergymen and other people of faith were imprisoned for their beliefs, and many lost their lives. Perhaps the most well-known of these German martyrs was Dietrich Bonhoeffer, a scholar and pastor who turned his back on the safety of a job as a professor in America so that he might return and fight against the evil he saw in the government of Adolf Hitler. He was hanged in 1945 for his involvement in trying to bring down that government, but while in prison he wrote *The Cost of Discipleship,* a treatise on the obligation of the person of faith in the face of injustice. Closer to home was Martin Luther King, Jr., who spent his life working tirelessly for the cause of justice in America for people of all races, and who was silenced in 1968 by an assassin's bullet. Archbishop Oscar Romero, serving the Roman Catholic Church in El Salvador during that country's civil war, spoke out on behalf of the poor of that country, advocating for the rights of peasants as God-given. For that he was assassinated in 1980.

It is easy to lionize these people as extraordinary, possessing a faith that is somehow superhuman. But while we may not be called upon to die for our faith, we are constantly called to make sacrifices as followers of Jesus. We may not lose our lives, but we may have to give up status, privilege, and power when we follow the gospel and ally ourselves with the persecuted. Like Campbell, we may find that leaving behind the comfort of the known opens for us a world rich in faith and experience, all for the love of God.

SCRIPTURE REFERENCES RELATED TO THE CHAPTER
Exodus 3:1–4:17
Matthew 5:23–25

DISCUSSION QUESTIONS

1. Is it possible to work for justice and peace while maintaining a position of social or political power for yourself? Why or why not?

2. What challenges do you face to live the gospel mandate of feeding the hungry, clothing the naked, releasing the captive, and caring for foreigners, widows, and orphans? What is the cost of your discipleship?

3. Martin Luther King, Jr., said, "There comes a time when one must take a position that is neither safe, nor politic, nor popular, but one must take it because it is right." Have you faced a choice between security and justice? Share with the group how you made the decision.

4. Dr. King was deeply committed to nonviolence as a way of life and as a means of resisting oppression. If you or your community were threatened with brutal violence, would you resist peacefully? Why or why not?

5. Moses posed four objections to God's call to a life of service (Exodus 3:1–4:17). What are they? Do you identify with any of Moses's objections?

6. Share with one another an experience of having been to the mountaintop and of seeing the Promised Land. How did this experience affect your life?

A GUIDE FOR PRAYER

1. Opening prayer

O God, who called the twelve to follow in the teachings of your Son, Jesus, give us strength and courage to follow him also in all that we do. In our work give us passion and a sense of justice for all who are oppressed, in our relationships give us honesty and a glimpse of your face in the other, in our prayers give us the strength of mind and heart to persevere and ask "thy will, not mine, be done." All this we ask through your Son, our savior, Jesus Christ. Amen.[9]

2. Scripture reading

Whoever loves father or mother more than me is not worthy of me; and whoever loves son or daughter more than me is not worthy of me; and whoever does not take up the cross and follow me is not worthy of me. Those who find their life will lose it, and those who lose their life for my sake will find it.

—MATTHEW 10:37–39

3. Question for reflection

This passage of paradoxes is challenging. What is God calling you to do through this passage?

4. Closing prayer

O God, who calls us to free the captive, help us to be like Moses and answer, "Here I am." When we deny that your Spirit lives in us, remind us that you are with us always. When we deny your holy name, remind us that we are yours. When we deny our authority, remind us that your hands and feet live through us. When we say we do not have the gifts to lead, remind us that it is not our work but yours alone. And when we deny that we are called, remind us of the words "Here I am."[10]

ACTIVITY

The Hebrew word *shalom* is commonly translated into English as *peace*. Shalom means much more than a world without conflict. Shalom expresses God's dream for wholeness, including right relationships and fullness of life and love among all God's creation. Pass out index cards and ask each person to write an adjective that describes God's vision for the world. Share your answers. What is shalom for today's weak and poor? What does shalom mean for the powerful and wealthy?

FINAL THOUGHTS

Based on the chapter and your exploration of it, what causes you sorrow? What inspires hope? What action might you take to address each?

Prodigals and the Path to Peace

THEME: RECONCILIATION

In the Gospel of John, Jesus is conversing with the disciples about his coming death. The disciples, as is so often the case, do not understand the words of their teacher, and finally, Jesus says, "You will know the truth, and the truth will make you free" (John 8:32). He continues by explaining that those who sin are forever slaves to their sins, and like slaves they have no permanent place in the family of believers. Unless they are willing and able to confess their transgressions, they will not have the love and comfort of knowing that they are rightful members of the household of God.

Campbell opens this chapter with the parable of the prodigal son (Luke 15:11–32), probably as well-known as that of the good Samaritan we examined in an earlier chapter. She focuses on the actions of the elder son, usually thought of as a marginal character in this story. He is filled with anger when he learns that his father has welcomed back the prodigal with feasting and celebration, and is unable to forgive either his returned brother or his father for what he sees as a failure to properly acknowledge the elder son's righteousness.

This parable calls to mind another one—that of the laborers in the vineyard (Matthew 20). A landowner hires workers to help tend his vineyard, agreeing to pay the usual daily rate. As the day progresses, he hires other workers to join in the labor. At the end of the day, he pays those who worked only a few hours the same daily wage he agreed to pay those who started very early. The workers who labored the longest revolt. The landowner points out that they are not being wronged, because they are receiving the wages they agreed to, and rebukes them for being envious of his generosity. So, we are told, it will be in the kingdom of God: the last will be first, and the first will be last.

Like the elder brother, we may find ourselves offended by this seeming unfairness. Shouldn't those who worked the hardest be rewarded for their labor? But this is a false perspective. The laborers hired earliest in the day, like the elder son who retains his inheritance, are not being punished; they receive all to which they are entitled.

When we look at the parable through the lens of the envy of the receiver, rather than through the lens of the seeming inequity of the giver, the truth of the matter becomes clear. Like greedy children, we focus on what our neighbor is getting, always on the lookout for slights. Jesus encourages us, instead, to keep our eyes firmly on our own sins rather than on the perceived sins of those around us. Just as the elder brother engaged in sins of envy and pride, we too can disregard the sins that enslave us because we are too busy cataloging the sins of others. In examining our own souls, and in asking for forgiveness, we see our own wrongs and are set free.

Campbell ends this chapter with a story of a white South African policeman who begs the forgiveness of President Kaunda of Zambia, whom he was supposed to kill. In the moment he seeks forgiveness, he is set free from his sin. He is set free from his enslavement to past wrongs and instead becomes a full member of the family of the new South Africa.

SCRIPTURE REFERENCES RELATED TO THE CHAPTER
Luke 15:11–32
2 Corinthians 5:12–21

DISCUSSION QUESTIONS
1. What might the parable of the forgiving father have to do with debt relief for developing countries?
2. What does the chapter suggest about the need for Americans to express remorse about the history of slavery in America? What else might Americans do to make reparations?

3. Undocumented workers, on average, earn less than legal workers and have fewer legal protections. Does their status have any similarity with that of slaves? What does your answer to this question imply for U.S. policy regarding undocumented workers?

4. What is the role of confession in your life? What new life has it brought to your commitment to justice?

5. Might there be circumstances when it is not appropriate to tell the truth? If so, when? If not, why?

6. What obstacles, cultural norms, or personal reservations keep you from sharing your fears and hopes with people unlike yourself?

7 What confessions need to be made in America to move toward reconciliation?

8. How does America's own experience of September 11, 2001, inform the need for truth and reconciliation?

A Guide for Prayer

1. Opening prayer

The hatred which divides nation from nation, race from race,
class from class,
O God, forgive.

The covetous desires of people and nations to possess what is
not their own,
O God, forgive.

The greed which exploits the labors of men and women and
lays waste the Earth,
O God, forgive.

Our envy of the welfare and happiness of others,
O God, forgive.

Our indifference to the plight of the homeless and the refugee,
O God, forgive.

The lust which dishonors the bodies of men, women, and
   children,
O God, forgive.

The pride that leads us to trust in ourselves and not in God,
O God, forgive.

Be kind to one another, tenderhearted, forgiving one another,
   as God in Christ forgave you.[11]

2. Scripture reading

Therefore, knowing the fear of the Lord, we try to persuade
others; but we ourselves are well-known to God, and I hope
that we are also well-known to your consciences. We are not
commending ourselves to you again, but giving you an
opportunity to boast about us, so that you may be able to
answer those who boast in outward appearance and not in
the heart. For if we are beside ourselves, it is for God; if we are
in our right mind, it is for you. For the love of Christ urges us
on, because we are convinced that one has died for all; therefore all have died. And he died for all, so that those who live
might live no longer for themselves, but for him who died and
was raised for them.

   From now on, therefore, we regard no one from a human
point of view; even though we once knew Christ from a human
point of view, we know him no longer in that way. So if anyone
is in Christ, there is a new creation: everything old has passed
away; see, everything has become new! All this is from God,
who reconciled us to himself through Christ, and has given us
the ministry of reconciliation; that is, in Christ God was recon-
ciling the world to himself, not counting their trespasses
against them, and entrusting the message of reconciliation to us.
So we are ambassadors for Christ, since God is making his appeal
through us; we entreat you on behalf of Christ, be reconciled

to God. For our sake he made him to be sin who knew no sin, so that in him we might become the righteousness of God.

−2 CORINTHIANS 5:11–21

3. Questions for reflection

What does it mean to be well-known by your conscience? How might the world be different if we did not count trespasses against one another?

4. Closing prayer

Gracious God, you create us and love us; you make us to live together in a community. We thank you for Martin Luther King, Jr., and all your children who have been filled with your vision for our lives and who have worked to bring your vision into reality. Fill us with your vision. Guide us to live by your vision, working to build the beloved community where everyone is welcomed, all are valued, power is shared, privilege is no more, and all your children know wholeness and well-being. Through Jesus Christ we pray. Amen.[12]

ACTIVITY

Watch the movie *Bamako* (directed by Abderrahmane Sissako, 2006), a film that weaves together the story of an African family in crisis with the trial by Africa against the World Bank and International Monetary Fund over the effects of their policies on African economies.

■ According to the movie, what roles have debt policy, stabilization, and trade liberalization played in the decline of economic welfare of most Africans?

■ What insights does the parable of the forgiving father offer to this problem?

FINAL THOUGHTS

Based on the chapter and your exploration of it, what causes you sorrow? What inspires hope? What action might you take to address each?

For Such a Time as This

THEME: CHOICES

In this chapter, Campbell reflects on the choices she has made and how these choices have shaped her life. She describes how one particular formative choice was marked by wrestling and uncertainty—and how at least one person advised against it. We all are shaped by the big and small choices we make daily. We choose careers, and life partners, and the issues with which we will passionately engage. Each choice closes a door and, in turn, opens up another constellation of choices. Sometimes our smallest choices shape our lives the most. The decision to drive rather than walk, for example, could lead to an unforeseen and life-changing accident.

Various spiritual traditions emphasize journaling as a way to keep track of the choices we make. By compiling a record of where we have been and where we find ourselves, we can look back over our choices and recognize patterns left undiscovered through simple remembering. Memory has a way of smoothing rough edges, subtly shifting details, reemphasizing some things over others.

Campbell details her decision to go to Belgrade during the NATO bombing of that city to negotiate for the release of three American soldiers taken as prisoners of war. She puts her own life at risk and is told by representatives of her own government that her mission is hopeless and that she and her group will be offered no protection. Despite this reality, Campbell and other faith leaders choose to risk their own safety to advocate for the release of these three soldiers. Ultimately, the trip is a success, and the prisoners are freed. But Campbell recognizes that the outcome could have been much different, and likens her own experience of choosing risk to that of Esther.

Because of her great beauty, Esther, a Jewish girl, captures the attention of the Persian king Ahasuerus, who offers her a chance to advocate for her people. Esther, though young, is clever and strong. She chooses to marry the king to spare her people from persecution. While she is ultimately triumphant, her triumph is not assured until the very end of her tale. At moments it looks as though she will fail. Still, she is driven by her conviction. To this day, she is a model of strength and valor because she was willing to sacrifice her own happiness to free her people. Like Campbell, she knew that making any other choice than to fight for those she loved would have haunted her for the rest of her days.

Esther's story is a dramatic example of high stakes and clear choices. In our own lives, though, we are more likely to find ourselves dealing with a series of smaller choices that seem insignificant but can determine the course of our lives. It is easy to decide without consideration, but if we keep God before us, even in the small choices, like Esther we will find in the end that we have lived lives of purpose.

SCRIPTURE REFERENCES RELATED TO THE CHAPTER
Esther 4:1–17

DISCUSSION QUESTIONS
1. What experiences have led to your interest in peace and reconciliation?
2. What does it mean to "stand by" someone who is unjustly treated? How does this act effect change?
3. More than two-thirds of all countries have abolished the death penalty. At fifty-two executions, the United States ranked fifth among all countries for the most executions in 2009. Does any crime justify execution? Why or why not?
4. What does it mean to be a messenger of the Divine?
5. How do wealth, security, and influence affect the choices you make?

A GUIDE FOR PRAYER

1. Opening prayer

Lord, make me an instrument of your peace;

where there is hatred, let me sow love;

where there is injury, pardon;

where there is doubt, faith;

where there is despair, hope;

where there is darkness, light;

where there is sadness, joy.

O divine Master,

grant that I may not so much seek to be consoled as to console;

to be understood, as to understand;

to be loved, as to love;

for it is in giving that we receive,

it is in pardoning that we are pardoned,

and it is in dying that we are born to eternal life.

Amen.

—ATTRIBUTED TO ST. FRANCIS OF ASSISI

2. Scripture reading

The Lord spoke to Moses on Mount Sinai, saying: Speak to the people of Israel and say to them: When you enter the land that I am giving you, the land shall observe a sabbath for the Lord. Six years you shall sow your field, and six years you shall prune your vineyard, and gather in their yield; but in the seventh year there shall be a sabbath of complete rest for the land, a sabbath for the Lord: you shall not sow your field or prune your vineyard. You shall not reap the aftergrowth of your harvest or gather the grapes of your unpruned vine: it shall be a year of complete rest for the land. You may eat what the land yields during its sabbath—you, your male and female slaves, your hired and your bound laborers who live with you; for your livestock also, and for the wild animals in your land all its yield shall be for food.

You shall count off seven weeks of years, seven times seven years, so that the period of seven weeks of years gives forty-nine years. Then you shall have the trumpet sounded loud; on the tenth day of the seventh month—on the day of atonement—you shall have the trumpet sounded throughout all your land. And you shall hallow the fiftieth year and you shall proclaim liberty throughout the land to all its inhabitants. It shall be a jubilee for you: you shall return, every one of you, to your property and every one of you to your family. That fiftieth year shall be a jubilee for you: you shall not sow, or reap the aftergrowth, or harvest the unpruned vines. For it is a jubilee; it shall be holy to you: you shall eat only what the field itself produces.

In this year of jubilee you shall return, every one of you, to your property. When you make a sale to your neighbor or buy from your neighbor, you shall not cheat one another. When you buy from your neighbor, you shall pay only for the number of years since the jubilee; the seller shall charge you only for the remaining crop years. If the years are more, you shall increase the price, and if the years are fewer, you shall diminish the price; for it is a certain number of harvests that are being sold to you. You shall not cheat one another, but you shall fear your God; for I am the Lord your God.

—Leviticus 25:1–17

3. Question for reflection

What meaning might the year of the jubilee have for us today?

4. Closing prayer

Now may the God of peace, who brought back from the dead our Lord Jesus, the great shepherd of the sheep, by the blood of the eternal covenant, make us complete in everything good so that we may do his will, working among us that which is pleasing in his sight, through Jesus Christ, to whom be the glory forever and ever. Amen.[13]

ACTIVITY

Ask each member of the group to take a piece of paper and draw a vertical line down the middle. List in one column the messengers—biblical and otherwise—and the messages they have conveyed to you in your lives. In the other column, list the actions you have taken to share that same message. When everyone is done, ask all the members to share one message they have proclaimed in their lives.

FINAL THOUGHTS

Based on the chapter and your exploration of it, what causes you sorrow? What inspires hope? What action might you take to address each?

The Beloved Community

THEME: HOPE

A saying attributed to many great theologians of our time goes like this: "The opposite of faith is not doubt, but fear." In this chapter, Campbell expands this statement by positing that the opposite of fear is hope; faith and hope go hand in hand. The early Christians who followed John, the beloved disciple of the Gospels, set their understanding of Jesus on living with love for all and hope for his return. Despite the harsh reality of living as a targeted group under the Roman occupation, they strove to maintain this hope and love in all their dealings with others, to bring about the reality of the kingdom of God on earth. It is easy to imagine how difficult this must have been. In the letter to the Romans, Paul encourages the community of Christians to persevere: "For in hope we were saved. Now hope that is seen is not hope. For who hopes for what is seen?" (Romans 8:24). To paraphrase: it isn't hoping if we are assured of success; it isn't faith if we are certain.

Campbell compares this early Christian model of hope with our own response, as a nation, to the horrors of the terrorist attacks of September 11, 2001. She notes that the tragedy gave us an opportunity to turn our country's great pain and loss into a beacon of hope for all those who were victims in the world—a truly biblical response to attack. Instead, we became prisoners of our own fear, lashing out blindly and setting in motion a chain of missteps and suffering throughout the world. Several years later, our country is still reeling from the events of that fall morning and has added countless thousands of dead, both our own and others, to the rolls of those killed that day.

Rabbi Jonathan Sacks, chief rabbi of the United Hebrew Congregations of the United Kingdom, said recently that if we want a model of true repentance, we need only look at the story of Joseph in the book of Genesis. After being almost murdered and then sold into slavery by his jealous brothers, Joseph works his way up to the position of viceroy in the court of the Egyptian pharaoh. Meanwhile, a great famine sweeps Joseph's homeland; only the Egyptians have grain. Joseph's brothers come before him, not recognizing the brother they had treated so harshly, and ask for food to sustain their community.

Through a complicated sequence of events, Joseph orders his brothers to leave their youngest brother, Benjamin, in his care as an assurance that they will return to pay for the grain he has given them. Judah, the brother who organized the plot against Joseph many years before, begs to be kept in place of the younger brother. As Judah reveals his fraternal love for Benjamin, Joseph reveals himself as the brother Judah and the others had abused many years before. What changed? Judah showed true repentance, Rabbi Sacks says, because he was presented with exactly the same circumstance years before—the opportunity to sacrifice a brother for his own benefit. This time he chose what was right. In that choice, in that example of repentance, Sacks finds hope for humanity. In the response of countless individual Americans on September 11, 2001, Campbell also found hope, and she continues to hope that, if as a nation we are faced again with the choices we faced in the aftermath of that act of terrorism, we would repent. This time we would choose love.

SCRIPTURE REFERENCES RELATED TO THE CHAPTER
Isaiah 65:17–25
John 15:1–17
John 21:15–19
Romans 8:18–30
Ephesians 4:4–6

DISCUSSION QUESTIONS
1. The theory of just war suggests circumstances under which war is legitimate, including 1) the cause is just, 2) the war is waged by a recognized authority, 3) the intention of the war is just, 4) a successful outcome is probable, 5) the means are proportionate to the ends, and

6) civilians are protected.[14] What are the arguments for and against just war? Do you think the Christian scriptures suggest a position with regard to just war?

2. Martin Luther King, Jr., and Mahatma Gandhi followed the principles of nonviolence to effect change in their countries. Both were assassinated. What does their success in addressing the ills of society have to say to the theory of just war?

3. What are the signs of love and hope in the Beloved Community? Why did you choose these signs? What are the challenges to establishing and sustaining these signs?

4. Read Isaiah 65:17–25 together. What is God's dream for the world? What actions can you take in your own community to live that dream?

5. How is a peacemaker different from a peacekeeper? Do both have legitimate roles in time of conflict? Are they complementary? Why or why not?

A Guide for Prayer

1. Opening prayer

(Divide into group A and group B. Say the following responsively.)

A: My soul magnifies the Lord,

B: and my spirit rejoices in God my Savior,

A: for he has looked with favor on the lowliness of his servant.

B: Surely, from now on all generations will call me blessed;

A: for the Mighty One has done great things for me,

B: and holy is his name.

A: His mercy is for those who fear him

B: from generation to generation.

A: He has shown strength with his arm;

B: he has scattered the proud in the thoughts of their hearts.

A: He has brought down the powerful from their thrones,

B: and lifted up the lowly;

A: he has filled the hungry with good things,

B: and sent the rich away empty.

A: He has helped his servant Israel,

B: in remembrance of his mercy,

A: according to the promise he made to our ancestors,

B: to Abraham and to his descendants forever.

—LUKE 1:46–55

2. Scripture reading

Jesus said:

Blessed are the peacemakers,

for they shall be known as the Children of God.

But I say to you that hear, love your enemies,

do good to those who hate you,

bless those who curse you,

pray for those who abuse you.

To those that strike you on the cheek,

offer the other one also,

and from those who take away your cloak,

do not withhold your coat as well.

Give to everyone who begs from you,

and of those who take away your goods,

do not ask for them again.

And as you wish that others would do to you,

do so to them.

—MATTHEW 5:9, 44, 39B–42; 7:12[15]

3. Question for reflection

How is there justice in blessing those who curse you and praying for those who abuse you?

4. Closing prayer

Mighty God, who causes the great wind, strong enough to
  split mountains,
Calm our hearts that we may know your loving presence.

God of power, who shakes the earth with rumbling and with
  fire,
Soothe our fear that we may set foot on the path of peace.

God of sheer silence, loud enough to deafen our ears,
Quiet our souls that we may look within and find the voice of
  justice.[16]

ACTIVITY

Watch *Hotel Rwanda* (Lions Gate Films, 2005) and explore the following
questions:

- How does Paul's sense of family change over the course of the
  movie?
- Jack does not believe that people will be moved to action even if
  they see the footage of the killings. Why might this be true?
- Paul made a choice between his immediate and his larger family.
  Did he make the right choice? Why or why not?

FINAL THOUGHTS

Based on the chapter and your exploration of it, what causes you sorrow?
What inspires hope? What action might you take to address each?

DISCUSSION GUIDE

The Road to Jerusalem

THEME: GOSPEL IMPERATIVES

In this chapter, Campbell offers the opportunity to reflect on selected gospel imperatives from the teachings of Jesus. In short, these are: 1) do not underrate the cost of the journey, 2) begin at the beginning, 3) claim the healing touch, 4) break down the barriers that divide, 5) forgive abundantly, 6) take up your cross, and 7) be open to God's surprises. All of these imperatives, taken together, encourage Christians to live beyond their own lives, to follow the new commandment of Jesus, and to love God, loving our neighbor as ourself. To emphasize her point, Campbell introduces this part of the book, "Faith in Action," by quoting from the letter of James:

> What good is it, my brothers and sisters, if you say you have faith but do not have works? Can faith save you? If a brother or sister is naked and lacks daily food, and one of you says to them, "Go in peace; keep warm and eat your fill," and yet you do not supply their bodily needs, what is the good of that? So faith by itself, if it has no works, is dead. But someone will say, "You have faith and I have works." Show me your faith apart from your works, and I by my works will show you my faith.
> —JAMES 2:14–18

Campbell's gospel imperatives are based in action, as her own life has been. It is tempting to live a silent witness to Jesus's word, to avoid the embarrassment of being thought a "holy roller" or "Jesus freak" by being good, polite people who keep their faith to themselves. But that is not the sort of witness the gospel calls us to. Like James, Campbell states that faith without works is dead. Faith without works can too quickly become simply an intellectual exercise. The faith Jesus modeled in his life was one of action and interaction.

157

It is only after we have worked with other believers to understand the gospel that we can talk about our experiences and our faith. We must follow the map until we have arrived at our destination. Similarly, we begin at the beginning. Following an African proverb, we undertake to clean the whole house by sweeping first at our feet. The task at hand may not be completed in our lifetimes, but that does not excuse us from getting the job started.

Throughout his ministry, Jesus healed others by laying hands on them. In calling us to use our own healing touch, Campbell challenges us to see the humanity of those who suffer and to connect with them as fellow children of God, because in that recognition dignity and love can exist. Doing so paves the way for breaking down barriers. Unity exists when we can see ourselves, and God, in one another, despite our differences in race, gender, class, or creed.

Jesus spent a significant portion of his ministry with those outside his own ethnic and religious group. We must do the same, always forgiving abundantly. For if we hold on to our resentments, we will never be able to work toward our positive goals. The weight we will carry, however, is that of the cross, as we must always be ready to choose hardship over comfort, what is right over what is easy. This Christian life of faith in action may sound daunting, but it is its own reward, and we can find all the courage and strength that we need to live it in the good news of Jesus.

SCRIPTURE REFERENCES RELATED TO THE CHAPTER
Psalm 139
Isaiah 42:1–4
Isaiah 61:1–2
Matthew 10:5–13
Matthew 10:34–42
Matthew 16:24–26
Matthew 26:36–46
Mark 10:46–52
Luke 1:78–80
Luke 4:14–40

Luke 22 and 23
John 13:35–14:7
John 15:13
John 17:18–22

Discussion Questions

1. God claimed Jesus's life to bring good news to the poor, to proclaim the release of captives, recovery of sight to the blind, and freedom to the oppressed. How has God claimed your life?
2. Find a photograph of trapeze artists in midair (a search engine is one way to find an image) and ask the following questions: What is the artist experiencing in that moment? What might go wrong? What surprises you? What is there to celebrate? How might this image be similar to or different from taking action to address issues of justice?
3. What example of Jesus's healing ministry is closest to your heart? Find it in the Gospels and read it together. What draws you to this story?
4. Those around blind Bartimaeus told him to keep quiet. Who are the naysayers in your life or community? Do any of their concerns make you reevaluate your decision? What response might you give to naysayers?
5. What does each of the seven guidelines suggested by the author mean to you?

A Guide for Prayer

1. Opening prayer

Open our hearts to see a new heaven and a new earth.
Refresh our spirits to feed the hungry.
Strengthen us to comfort those who weep.
Grant us compassion to minister to the poor.
Ignite a fire in our hearts to advocate for the needy.
Open our eyes to the abundance you have given us to share.
Embolden our resolve to live into the new heaven and the new earth.[17]

2. Scripture reading

They came to Jericho. As he and his disciples and a large crowd were leaving Jericho, Bartimaeus son of Timaeus, a blind beggar, was sitting by the roadside. When he heard that it was Jesus of Nazareth, he began to shout out and say, "Jesus, Son of David, have mercy on me!" Many sternly ordered him to be quiet, but he cried out even more loudly, "Son of David, have mercy on me!" Jesus stood still and said, "Call him here." And they called the blind man, saying to him, "Take heart; get up, he is calling you." So throwing off his cloak, he sprang up and came to Jesus. Then Jesus said to him, "What do you want me to do for you?" The blind man said to him, "My teacher, let me see again." Jesus said to him, "Go; your faith has made you well." Immediately he regained his sight and followed him on the way.

—MARK 10:46–52

3. Questions for reflection

If it was clear Bartimaeus was blind, why did Jesus ask him, "What do you want me to do for you?"

What does Jesus's question suggest for your life?

4. Closing prayer

Give the king your justice, O God,
> and your righteousness to a king's son.
May he judge your people with righteousness,
> and your poor with justice.
May the mountains yield prosperity for the people,
> and the hills, in righteousness.
May he defend the cause of the poor of the people,
> give deliverance to the needy,
> and crush the oppressor.

—PSALM 72:1–4

ACTIVITY

The author suggests this guide to the journey: "Begin at the beginning." Ask participants to write a brief spiritual autobiography, beginning by listing three important events in their spiritual lives. Continue by answering this question for each event: how has this event formed who I am today?

FINAL THOUGHTS

Based on the chapter and your exploration of it, what causes you sorrow? What inspires hope? What action might you take to address each?

Dangerous Dreams

THEME: COMPASSION

A novice in a monastery was talking to the superior of the order about his first year there: "I wake every morning before sunrise and spend three hours reading the holy scriptures. I then pray for three hours, and eat only a crust of moldy bread for my morning meal. I spend the rest of the daylight in the chapel on my hands and knees reciting the psalms, eat another crust of bread in the evening hours, and spend the rest of the night reading scripture. I drink only a half-cup of water, and I sleep for only three hours, and then I begin again with the same routine." The superior considered this grueling regimen, and then asked a single question, "In doing these things do you increase your compassion for your fellow human being?" The novice was stunned into silence. "Then it is all for nothing," the superior said. "Go back, and begin again."

This story, handed down in the oral religious tradition, illustrates our ability, as individuals and as people of faith, to get caught up in the details of religious life to the detriment of our greater calling. Like the eager young novice, we are quick to fast and engage in disciplined spiritual practices, but slower to notice whether our minds and hearts are being changed by the work of our bodies. As Campbell notes in this chapter, and as the wise superior pointed out to the novice, without compassion for our brothers and sisters, fasting, praying, and faithful observance are all for nothing.

How do we manifest compassion, particularly in our work with people from other faith traditions? How do we, as Christians, Jews, or Muslims, stay true to our own beliefs while also respecting and engaging in dialogue with those of other faiths? The World Council of Churches addressed this very issue for Christian leaders in its 1989 consensus statement on the relation between Christianity and other religions. The consensus can be summarized in three sentences: "We cannot point to any other way of salvation than Jesus Christ; at the same time we cannot put any limit to God's saving power. There is a tension between these affirmations which we acknowledge and cannot resolve."[18]

In his book *Acts of Faith*, interfaith activist and scholar Eboo Patel describes how his own experience growing up as an Indian Muslim in America shaped the mission of the Interfaith Youth Core (IFYC), an organization he directs in Chicago. The purpose of the IFYC is to introduce young people from different faiths to each other through service and outreach, so that the risk of radical fundamentalism in any tradition is arrested through friendships.

Patel acknowledges that the Jews, Muslims, Christians, Hindus, Buddhists, Sikhs, and followers of other faiths represented in the IFYC sometimes differ greatly in their beliefs, and the organization says those competing theological claims simply have to be respectfully accepted. The program focuses on the shared values of all of these faiths—hospitality, cooperation, mercy, and compassion. In coming together around these shared values, young people discuss how their individual faiths address their values through their own paths, and in teaching each other to develop their own faith identities. Patel describes this as "affirming particularity and achieving pluralism."[19] It is also a surefire recipe for developing compassion.

Sweeping generalizations made by one religion about the followers of another can be defused instantly with the memory of a friend who happens to belong to that other religion, and who does not resemble that generalization at all. In this simple building of relationships that cross religious lines, community is created, and compassion is assured. We look to the youth of our increasingly global culture to make these dreams of unity a reality.

SCRIPTURE REFERENCES RELATED TO THE CHAPTER
John 10:11–18
John 17
Hebrews 11:1
Revelation 21:1–6

Discussion Questions

1. The Greek word for compassion literally means to feel from one's bowels, the depth of one's being. Feeling from the depth of one's being requires putting yourself in the position of the other. How does this understanding of the word *compassion* change or affirm your understanding of interfaith dialogue?

2. How do you understand Revelation 21:6, "I am the Alpha and Omega, the beginning and the end," in today's pluralistic society?

3. The Golden Rule is also called "reciprocity ethics." What Golden Rules do you know from the world's religions? Does calling it "reciprocity ethics" change its meaning? How? Or why not?

4. What do you mean by *faith*? Compare your definition with the meaning in Hebrews 11:1. What insight do you gain from the comparison?

5. Do you, or does your community, have any dangerous dreams? What makes them dangerous?

A Guide for Prayer

1. Opening prayer

Ever-creating God, whose property is always to have mercy: give us the grace to deal justly with all your children, to have compassion upon those who walk this holy pilgrimage of life with us, and to seek to serve you in every interaction, that we may be faithful members of your heavenly kingdom. Amen.[20]

2. Scripture reading

Comfort, O comfort my people,
 says your God.
Speak tenderly to Jerusalem,
 and cry to her
that she has served her term,
 that her penalty is paid,

that she has received from the Lord's hand
    double for all her sins.
A voice cries out:
"In the wilderness prepare the way of the Lord,
    make straight in the desert a highway for our God.
Every valley shall be lifted up,
    and every mountain and hill be made low;
the uneven ground shall become level,
    and the rough places a plain.
Then the glory of the Lord shall be revealed,
    and all people shall see it together,
    for the mouth of the Lord has spoken."
                      —ISAIAH 40:1–5

3. Questions for reflection

The Hebrew word for comfort is *nachamu* (pronounced *na-kha moo*), which means to console or have compassion. What are the implications of this definition for this passage in Isaiah? What is the prophet called to do?

The English word *comfort* comes from Latin *confortare*, meaning "to strengthen." What insight does this provide for the reading?

4. Closing prayer

Almighty God, we give you thanks for the gift of compassion, that we may see you in all those we meet. Help us to work for unity in your name, and to struggle always for justice and peace and what is right. Keep ever-present in our hearts the love you have for the whole world. Amen.[21]

ACTIVITY

Watch and discuss the movie *Acting on Faith: Women's New Religious Activism in America* (Rachel Antell and the Pluralism Project, 2005). This documentary looks at the lives and work of three American women of different faiths—Buddhism, Hinduism, and Islam—and how their faiths inform their identities and actions in the world. Discuss the following questions:

- How does your faith affect the lens through which you see the world?
- How does this lens differ from how others (atheists, Jews, Muslims, Hindus, Sikhs) see the world?

A study guide with additional questions for discussion is available at www.pluralism.org/affiliates/antell/StudyGuide.pdf.

FINAL THOUGHTS

Based on the chapter and your exploration of it, what causes you sorrow? What inspires hope? What action might you take to address each?

Science and Religion

Theme: Sacred Creation

What is the responsibility of a Christian to the world that God has created? Campbell argues in this chapter that as people of God, we must love the earth and protect it, we must advocate for it in our laws and in our practices, and we must be stewards worthy of the responsibility and the gift God gave us when this wonderful "pale blue dot" was given to us as our home. This has not always been the Christian perspective on environmental stewardship. Even now some groups that call themselves Christian advocate spending down the earth's resources in a planned destruction of this island home of ours to force God's hand and bring about the end times. Most people of faith, though, seek to preserve God's creation from the misdeeds of human beings.

Our story as the people of God began in a garden filled with the wonders of the natural world. The animals and creeping things were given to us to name and nurture, and we are told in Genesis that God delighted in walking in the cool of evening with Adam and Eve, admiring the beauty of creation. We are told that it was the failure of those original human beings to obey God's rules regarding the use of these resources (in that case, eating the fruit of the tree of the knowledge of good and evil) resulted in our expulsion from that heaven on earth, and it is difficult not to view our current abuses of the natural world as repeating that offense.

Our understanding of the science of the natural world is only a few centuries old. Research and technology have developed our knowledge of natural processes and the ways they are interrupted by our own acts—especially in the last few decades. Battle lines that were drawn early in our modern history between scientists and people of faith have contributed to deep distrust by both camps, even while many people of faith also appreciate the work of scientists.

Quoting Carl Sagan's "Open Letter to the Religious Community," Campbell agrees that "efforts to safeguard and cherish the environment need to be infused with a vision of the sacred," lest we all find ourselves without a home. It is not uncommon for a Christian to reflect on a particularly beautiful sunset or a powerful thunderstorm as a moment when not only God's existence, but God's love of creation, seems certain. The Psalms act as an extended metaphor comparing the beauty of the natural world to the depth and breadth of God's love and care for us (Psalms 8, 19, and 139, to cite but a few), and the Song of Solomon revels in the beauty of the human body, lovingly created by God for God's beloved humanity. How, with that biblical witness, can we as people of this earth have anything but love and care for our world? As Campbell notes, this "pale blue dot" as viewed from space is the womb in which we were formed with care and love, the breast at which we are nurtured. It is the garden created for us to live in, enjoying the cool of the evening breeze, walking hand in hand with our God.

SCRIPTURE REFERENCES RELATED TO THE CHAPTER
Psalm 8
Genesis 1:1–2:4
Genesis 12:1–3
Leviticus 25:1–24
Psalm 104

DISCUSSION QUESTIONS
1. A basic way of understanding the economy is the cost/benefit model. In this model, people make decisions based on whether the marginal benefit exceeds the marginal cost. Within this framework, the cost of reducing pollution is higher than its benefit. How might this model inform public debate about pollution? How might this model be flawed?
2. Stephen J. Gould, American paleontologist, evolutionary biologist, and historian of science, asserts:

The net of science covers the empirical universe: what is it made of (fact) and why does it work this way (theory). The net of religion extends over questions of moral meaning and value. These two magisteria do not overlap, nor do they encompass all inquiry (consider, for starters, the magisterium of art and the meaning of beauty). To cite the arch cliches, we get the age of rocks, and religion retains the rock of ages; we study how the heavens go, and they determine how to go to heaven.[22]

Do you agree or disagree with this theory of the distinctions between science and religion? Share your reasons with one another. What impact does your answer have on the conversation about the environment?

3. The author uses the phrase "crimes against creation" to describe actions that harm the environment. Research scientists at the Fisheries Center of the University of British Columbia claim that human "interactions with fisheries resources have come to resemble … wars of extermination."[23] They are referring to the rapid depletion of sea life caused by overfishing. How might using this language change people's responses to environmental issues?

4. How are science and religion different ways of knowing reality? In your opinion, are these ways complementary or mutually exclusive?

5. How much of our care for the environment is (or ought to be) motivated by the continuation of human life? What other motivations exist? Consider both religious and secular reasons.

A Guide for Prayer

1. Opening prayer

For the beauty of the earth,
For the beauty of the skies,
For the Love which from our birth
Over and around us likes:
Christ, our God, to Thee we raise
This our Sacrifice of Praise.[24]

2. Scripture reading

And God said, "Let the waters under the sky be gathered together into one place, and let the dry land appear." And it was so. God called the dry land Earth, and the waters that were gathered together he called Seas. And God saw that it was good. Then God said, "Let the earth put forth vegetation: plants yielding seed, and fruit trees of every kind on earth that bear fruit with the seed in it." And it was so. The earth brought forth vegetation: plants yielding seed of every kind, and trees of every kind bearing fruit with the seed in it. And God saw that it was good. And there was evening and there was morning, the third day....

Then God said, "Let us make humankind in our image, according to our likeness; and let them have dominion over the fish of the sea, and over the birds of the air, and over the cattle, and over all the wild animals of the earth, and over every creeping thing that creeps upon the earth."

So God created humankind in his image,
in the image of God he created them;
male and female he created them.

God blessed them, and God said to them, "Be fruitful and multiply, and fill the earth and subdue it; and have dominion over the fish of the sea and over the birds of the air and over every living thing that moves upon the earth." God said, "See, I have given you every plant yielding seed that is upon the face of all the earth, and every tree with seed in its fruit; you shall have them for food. And to every beast of the earth, and to every bird of the air, and to everything that creeps on the earth, everything that has the breath of life, I have given every green plant for food." And it was so. God saw everything that he had made, and indeed, it was very good. And there was evening and there was morning, the sixth day.

—Genesis 1:9–13, 26–31

3. Questions for reflection

The reading pairs the third with the sixth day of creation. What does this pairing suggest about God's desires for the relationship between the earth's resources and its inhabitants? What does the reading suggest about our call to stewardship?

4. Closing prayer

Almighty and everlasting God, you made the universe with all its marvelous order, its atoms, worlds, and galaxies, and the infinite complexity of living creatures: Grant that, as we probe the mysteries of your creation, we may come to know you more truly, and more surely fulfill our role in your eternal purpose; in the name of Jesus Christ our Lord. Amen.[25]

ACTIVITY

The number of environmental refugees (people displaced due to environmental degradation) is expected to rise in the coming decades. The majority of these refugees will be from developing countries.

- What does your faith suggest as a response to this problem?
- What biblical stories support these actions? (Examples are Exodus 18:1–18; Genesis 42–45; Ruth; Deuteronomy 24:19–21; Matthew 25:31–46.) Choose one and read it. What insight does it offer to this problem?
- What might your group do to raise awareness of this issue?
- What individual and congregational action might you take to reduce your negative impact on the environment?

FINAL THOUGHTS

Based on the chapter and your exploration of it, what causes you sorrow? What inspires hope? What action might you take to address each?

On Prayer

THEME: CONVERSATIONS WITH GOD

Campbell describes prayer in her life as a way of talking to God, of having a conversation that looks not for results but for life lessons. She also finds in prayer a source of strength and wisdom.

The definitions of prayer are as varied as the prayers we pray each day, in moments of anxiety or moments of joy. Writer Anne Lamott says the two best prayers she knows are: "Help me, help me, help me" and "Thank you, thank you, thank you."[26] In the catechism found in the *Book of Common Prayer* used by Episcopalians, prayer is defined as "responding to God, by thought and by deeds, with or without words."[27]

Other Christian denominations and other faiths may approach prayer differently, with some praying only corporately, that is, with a body of other faithful believers, and some praying only individually. The prayer of the yogis of some branches of Hinduism takes a physical form and is described in the postures of the body and the rhythm of breath. The whirling dervishes of Sufi Islam are a familiar example of actively engaging the body and mind in praise of God. Some Buddhists build prayer wheels to use in their meditation practice, just as some Christians walk labyrinths to involve both their bodies and minds in the act of prayer, or pray with rosaries or other beads. Some Jews think of doing a *mitzvah* as praying. *Mitzvah*, translated from Hebrew, literally means commandment, and refers to the 613 commandments, or laws, of Judaism found in the Torah. Some Jews define a *mitzvah* as an act of kindness. Whenever a Jew performs a *mitzvah*, God is praised.

As Christians, we have an example in the prayer Jesus taught his disciples in Matthew 6:9–13 and in Luke 11:2–4, a prayer many of us learned as children, whether we called it the Lord's Prayer or Our Father. Regardless of the form or words we use, it is important that we pray, because prayer nourishes our souls much as food nourishes our bodies.

The act of praying gives us sacred space set aside from our daily secular responsibilities to imagine ourselves as God sees us and to rest, when weary, in the safety and peace of God's arms.

SCRIPTURE REFERENCES RELATED TO THE CHAPTER

Matthew 6:9–13

Luke 18:1

Philippians 4:6–7

DISCUSSION QUESTIONS

1. What prayer in your life remains unanswered? What signs of hope might glimmer in the future?
2. When do you find it easy to pray? When is prayer difficult?
3. What type of prayer are you most comfortable with? How might you expand your prayer life?
4. What are the characteristics of the America you dream about?
5. What legacies of our American forefathers and foremothers would you like to cast aside? What would you like to take forward?
6. How do you describe freedom? What are its privileges? What are its responsibilities?
7. Campbell shares that music often opens her to prayer. What opens you to prayer?

A GUIDE FOR PRAYER

1. Opening prayer

Creator God, who knows our every thought and action, sustain us with your Spirit that we may do your bidding in this world. Comfort us so that we might comfort others. Heal us so that we can offer your healing grace. Nourish us so that we can go out into the world, sharing the good news of Christ. We ask this in the name of your Son, Jesus Christ, our Lord and only Savior. Amen.[28]

2. Scripture reading

Pray then in this way:
Our Father in heaven,
    hallowed be your name.
Your kingdom come.
Your will be done,
    on earth as it is in heaven.
Give us this day our daily bread.
And forgive us our debts,
    as we also have forgiven our debtors.
And do not bring us to the time of trial,
    but rescue us from the evil one.

—MATTHEW 6:9–13

3. Questions for reflection

What does the writer of Matthew emphasize in his version of the prayer given by Jesus?

How has this prayer formed your actions today?

4. Closing prayer

May the beckoning light of the new day call us to praise you in the morning.

May the height of the sun lift us to serve you at noon.

May the folding of the day wrap us in your love toward a restful night.

Amen.[29]

ACTIVITY

Many of the psalms are written in couplets, two-line groupings in which the second line completes, contrasts, or extends the thought of the first line.

Write a group psalm. The first person writes line one and passes the page with that line to person two. This second person writes a one-line response to the first person. The third person begins a new thought and the process continues. A psalm often begins by addressing God and continues with a complaint followed by what the petitioner will do for God, or praise for God.

FINAL THOUGHTS

Based on the chapter and your exploration of it, what causes you sorrow? What inspires hope? What action might you take to address each?

About the Discussion Guide Authors

A popular speaker, retreat leader, and workshop presenter on the topics of spirituality, prayer, and teen faith formation, **Jenifer Gamber** has been involved in Christian formation since she began teaching Sunday school as a teenager. She is the author of two widely read books about religious formation: *My Faith, My Life* for teenagers and *Your Faith, Your Life* for adults. Her website, www.myfaithmylife.org, offers a wealth of resources for adults who work with youth. She is the vice president of the National Association for Episcopal Christian Education Directors, and has an active ministry leading confirmation and baptism preparation at her home church, the Cathedral Church of the Nativity in Bethlehem, Pennsylvania.

Reverend Canon Mariclair Partee was born and raised in Atlanta, Georgia. After a career as a labor and employment lawyer in Atlanta, she attended the General Theological Seminary of the Episcopal Church in New York and was ordained an Episcopal priest. She has worked for the Episcopal Church's Office of Ecumenical and Interfaith Relations and currently serves as the canon for the Ministry of the Baptized at the Cathedral Church of the Nativity in the Diocese of Bethlehem, Pennsylvania, where she is also a member of the diocesan Commission for Ecumenical and Interfaith Relations.

Notes

Introduction

1. From the PBS *Frontline* documentary "From Jesus to Christ: The First Christians—Part II," April 7, 1998, www.pbs.org/wgbh/pages/frontline/shows/religion/etc/script2.html.

Love Matters

1. Silvia Pedraza, *Political Disaffection in Cuba's Revolution and Exodus* (New York: Cambridge University Press, 2007), 5.

Bearing Down in Love

1. Speech given by Abraham Lincoln on June 16, 1858, at the Illinois State Republican Convention upon his nomination for the Senate seat. Lincoln ran unsuccessfully against Stephen Douglas.

2. "Number of Americans in Poverty Up Slightly," *CBS News*, August 26, 2008, www.cbsnews.com/stories/2008/08/26/national/main4384762.shtml.

3. From a sermon preached in 1956 at Dexter Avenue Church in Chicago, quoted in Martin Luther King, Jr., *Strength to Love* (Minneapolis: Fortress Press, 2010), 56.

Who Is My Neighbor?

1. John Wesley, *The Works of John Wesley*, vol. 19, *Journal and Diaries II, 1738–1743*, ed. W. Reginald Ward and Richard P. Heitzenrater (Nashville: Abingdon Press, 1990), 67.

One Shepherd, One Flock

1. Martin Luther King, Jr., *A Testament of Hope: The Essential Writings and Speeches of Martin Luther King, Jr.*, ed. James M. Washington (New York: HarperCollins, 1986), 286.

Sacred Conversation

1. King, *Testament of Hope*, 243.

Prodigals and the Path to Peace

1. Pope John Paul II, "Reconciliation and Penance," post-synodal apostolic exhortation, Rome, December 2, 1984.

For Such a Time as This

1. For an article on this incident in which the author is quoted, see Howard Chua-Eoan, "Mission Improbable," May 3, 1999, www.cnn.com/ALLPOLITICS/time/1999/05/03/ jackson.html.
2. Robert Frost, "The Road Not Taken," in *Mountain Interval* (New York: Henry Holt, 1921), 9.

The Beloved Community

1. Martin Luther King, Jr., *Strength to Love*, 47.
2. Martin Luther King, Jr., "Loving Your Enemies," a sermon delivered at Dexter Avenue Baptist Church, Montgomery, Alabama, November 17, 1957.
3. Martin Luther King, Jr., "Loving Your Enemies."
4. From an inaugural address given in 1989, in which Havel paraphrased the seventeenth-century theologian Comemius.
5. Adapted from a prayer by the author for a board of trustees meeting at Chautauqua Institution, February 4, 2010.

Dangerous Dreams

1. Madeleine Korbel Albright, *The Mighty and the Almighty: Reflections on America, God, and World Affairs* (New York: HarperCollins, 2006).
2. "Charter for Compassion," www.charterforcompassion.org.

Science and Religion

1. Langdon Gilkey, *Creationism on Trial: Evolution and God at Little Rock* (Minneapolis: Winston Press, 1985), 99–100.
2. Gilkey, *Creationism on Trial*, 122.

3. James M. Gustafson, "Faithfulness: Remembering H. Richard Niebuhr," *Christian Century*, October 5, 1994, 885.
4. First published in Yervant Terzian and Elizabeth Bilson, eds., *Carl Sagan's Universe* (New York: Cambridge University Press, 1997), 254–260.

On Prayer
1. Delivered June 19, 2007, Chautauqua, New York.
2. Delivered fall 2008, Chautauqua, New York.
3. Delivered July 4, 2010, Chautauqua, New York.

Discussion Guide
1. Reverend Ann K. Fontaine.
2. Ibid.
3. Jenifer Gamber.
4. William Law, as quoted in 2000 *Years of Prayer*, comp. Michael Counsell (Harrisburg, Pa.: Morehouse, 1999), 307–308.
5. "Collect for the Human Family," in *The Book of Common Prayer* (New York: Church Hymnal Corporation, 1979), 815.
6. This series of questions is based on questions designed for a program of theological reflection called Education for Ministry, whose headquarters are at the University of the South.
7. "Worship Resources Inspired by the Belhar Confession" booklet (New York: Reformed Church Press, 2009).
8. Ellen Bradshaw Aitken, *Loosening the Roots of Compassion: Meditations for Holy Week and Eastertide* (Cambridge, Mass.: Cowley, 2006), 12.
9. Mariclair Partee.
10. Jenifer Gamber.
11. Prayer of the Community of the Cross of Nails, prayed at Coventry Cathedral, England, at the altar of reconciliation every Friday at noon.
12. Mark Koenig, "Closing Prayer," *Martin Luther King Jr. Day Worship Resources*, Presbyterian Peacemaking Program, http://archive.pcusa.org/peacemaking/worship/mlk.htm.
13. Hebrews 13:20–21, adapted.
14. Alexander Moseley, "Just War Theory," *The Internet Encyclopedia of Philosophy*, 2009, www.iep.utm.edu/justwar.
15. St. Paul's Chapel, "Prayers for Peace and Reconciliation" booklet (New York: St. Paul's Chapel, n.d.), www.saintpaulschapel.org/PrayersForPeace.pdf.
16. Jenifer Gamber.

17. Ibid.
18. World Council of Churches, "History of World Mission and Evangelism," www.oikoumene.org/en/who-are-we/organization-structure/consultative-bodies/world-mission-and-evangelism/history.html.
19. Eboo Patel, *Acts of Faith: The Story of an American Muslim, the Struggle for the Soul of a Generation* (Boston: Beacon Press, 2008), 167.
20. Mariclair Partee.
21. Ibid.
22. Stephen J. Gould, "Nonoverlapping Magisteria," *Natural History Magazine* 106 (March 1997): 88; www.stephenjaygould.org/library/gould_noma.html.
23. As quoted in Jonathan Safran Foer, *Eating Animals* (New York: Little, Brown, 2009), 33.
24. Folliot S. Pierpoint, *Lyra Eucharistica*, 2nd ed., ed. Orby Shipley (London: Longman, Green, Longman, Roberts, and Green, 1864), 340.
25. "Prayer for the Knowledge of God's Creation," *Book of Common Prayer*, 827.
26. Anne Lamott, *Traveling Mercies: Some Thoughts on Faith* (New York: Pantheon Books, 1999), 82.
27. *Book of Common Prayer*, 856.
28. Jenifer Gamber.
29. Ibid.

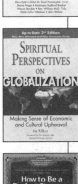

Judaism / Christianity / Islam / Interfaith

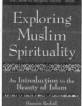

Exploring Muslim Spirituality: An Introduction to the Beauty of Islam
by Hussein Rashid Moves beyond basic information to explore what Islam means to a believer—written by a believer. 6 x 9, 192 pp (est), Quality PB, 978-1-59473-277-5 **$16.99**

Getting to the Heart of Interfaith
The Eye-Opening, Hope-Filled Friendship of a Pastor, a Rabbi and a Sheikh
by Pastor Don Mackenzie, Rabbi Ted Falcon and Sheikh Jamal Rahman
Offers many insights and encouragements for individuals and groups who want to tap into the promise of interfaith dialogue. 6 x 9, 192 pp, Quality PB, 978-1-59473-263-8 **$16.99**

Hearing the Call across Traditions: Readings on Faith and Service
Edited by Adam Davis; Foreword by Eboo Patel Explores the connections between faith, service and social justice through the prose, verse and sacred texts of the world's great faith traditions. 6 x 9, 352 pp, HC, 978-1-59473-264-5 **$29.99**

How to Do Good & Avoid Evil: A Global Ethic from the Sources of Judaism *by Hans Küng and Rabbi Walter Homolka; Translated by Rev. Dr. John Bowden* Explores how Judaism's ethical principles can help all religions work together toward a more peaceful humankind. 6 x 9, 224 pp, HC, 978-1-59473-255-3 **$19.99**

Blessed Relief: What Christians Can Learn from Buddhists about Suffering
by Gordon Peerman 6 x 9, 208 pp, Quality PB, 978-1-59473-252-2 **$16.99**

The Changing Christian World: A Brief Introduction for Jews
by Rabbi Leonard A. Schoolman 5½ x 8½, 176 pp, Quality PB, 978-1-58023-344-6 **$16.99***

Christians & Jews in Dialogue: Learning in the Presence of the Other *by Mary C. Boys and Sara S. Lee; Foreword by Dorothy C. Bass* 6 x 9, 240 pp, Quality PB, 978-1-59473-254-6 **$18.99**; HC, 978-1-59473-144-0 **$21.99**

Disaster Spiritual Care: Practical Clergy Responses to Community, Regional and National Tragedy *Edited by Rabbi Stephen B. Roberts, BCJC, and Rev. Willard W.C. Ashley, Sr., DMin, DH* 6 x 9, 384 pp, HC, 978-1-59473-240-9 **$40.00**

InterActive Faith: The Essential Interreligious Community-Building Handbook
Edited by Rev. Bud Heckman with Rori Picker Neiss; Foreword by Rev. Dirk Ficca
6 x 9, 304 pp, HC, 978-1-59473-237-9 **$29.99**

The Jewish Approach to God: A Brief Introduction for Christians
by Rabbi Neil Gillman, PhD 5½ x 8½, 192 pp, Quality PB, 978-1-58023-190-9 **$16.95***

The Jewish Approach to Repairing the World (*Tikkun Olam*): A Brief Introduction for Christians *by Rabbi Elliot N. Dorff, PhD, with Rev. Cory Willson*
5½ x 8½, 256 pp, Quality PB, 978-1-58023-349-1 **$16.99***

The Jewish Connection to Israel, the Promised Land: A Brief Introduction for Christians *by Rabbi Eugene Korn, PhD* 5½ x 8½, 192 pp, Quality PB, 978-1-58023-318-7 **$14.99***

Jewish Holidays: A Brief Introduction for Christians *by Rabbi Kerry M. Olitzky and Rabbi Daniel Judson* 5½ x 8½, 176 pp, Quality PB, 978-1-58023-302-6 **$16.99***

Jewish Ritual: A Brief Introduction for Christians
by Rabbi Kerry M. Olitzky and Rabbi Daniel Judson 5½ x 8½, 144 pp, Quality PB, 978-1-58023-210-4 **$14.99***

Jewish Spirituality: A Brief Introduction for Christians *by Rabbi Lawrence Kushner* 5½ x 8½, 112 pp, Quality PB, 978-1-58023-150-3 **$12.95***

A Jewish Understanding of the New Testament *by Rabbi Samuel Sandmel; New preface by Rabbi David Sandmel* 5½ x 8½, 368 pp, Quality PB, 978-1-59473-048-1 **$19.99***

Modern Jews Engage the New Testament: Enhancing Jewish Well-Being in a Christian Environment *by Rabbi Michael J. Cook, PhD* 6 x 9, 416 pp, HC 978-1-58023-313-2 **$29.99***

Talking about God: Exploring the Meaning of Religious Life with Kierkegaard, Buber, Tillich and Heschel *by Daniel F. Polish, PhD* 6 x 9, 160 pp, Quality PB, 978-1-59473-272-0 **$16.99**

We Jews and Jesus: Exploring Theological Differences for Mutual Understanding
by Rabbi Samuel Sandmel; New preface by Rabbi David Sandmel
6 x 9, 192 pp, Quality PB, 978-1-59473-208-9 **$16.99**

Who Are the *Real* Chosen People? The Meaning of Chosenness in Judaism, Christianity and Islam *by Reuven Firestone, PhD*
6 x 9, 176 pp, Quality PB, 978-1-59473-290-4 **$16.99**

* A book from Jewish Lights, SkyLight Paths' sister imprint

Spirituality

Creative Aging: Rethinking Retirement and Non-Retirement in a Changing World *by Marjory Zoet Bankson*
Offers creative ways to nourish our calling and discover meaning and purpose in our older years.   6 x 9, 160 pp, Quality PB, 978-1-59473-281-2 **$16.99**

Laugh Your Way to Grace: Reclaiming the Spiritual Power of Humor
by Rev. Susan Sparks   A powerful, humorous case for laughter as a spiritual, healing path.   6 x 9, 176 pp, Quality PB, 978-1-59473-280-5 **$16.99**

Living into Hope: A Call to Spiritual Action for Such a Time as This
by Rev. Dr. Joan Brown Campbell; Foreword by Karen Armstrong
A visionary minister speaks out on the pressing issues that face us today, offering inspiration and challenge.   6 x 9, 144 pp (est), HC, 978-1-59473-283-6 **$21.99**

Claiming Earth as Common Ground: The Ecological Crisis through the Lens of Faith *by Andrea Cohen-Kiener; Foreword by Rev. Sally Bingham*
Inspires us to work across denominational lines in order to fulfill our sacred imperative to care for God's creation.   6 x 9, 192 pp, Quality PB, 978-1-59473-261-4 **$16.99**

Bread, Body, Spirit: Finding the Sacred in Food
Edited and with Introductions by Alice Peck   6 x 9, 224 pp, Quality PB, 978-1-59473-242-3 **$19.99**

Creating a Spiritual Retirement: A Guide to the Unseen Possibilities in Our Lives
by Molly Srode   6 x 9, 208 pp, b/w photos, Quality PB, 978-1-59473-050-4 **$14.99**

Finding Hope: Cultivating God's Gift of a Hopeful Spirit
by Marcia Ford; Foreword by Andrea Jaeger   8 x 8, 176 pp, Quality PB, 978-1-59473-211-9 **$16.99**

Hearing the Call across Traditions: Readings on Faith and Service
Edited by Adam Davis; Foreword by Eboo Patel   6 x 9, 352 pp, HC, 978-1-59473-264-5 **$29.99**

Honoring Motherhood: Prayers, Ceremonies & Blessings
Edited and with Introductions by Lynn L. Caruso   5 x 7¼, 272 pp, HC, 978-1-59473-239-3 **$19.99**

Journeys of Simplicity: Traveling Light with Thomas Merton, Bashō, Edward Abbey, Annie Dillard & Others *by Philip Harnden*
5 x 7¼, 144 pp, Quality PB, 978-1-59473-181-5 **$12.99**; 128 pp, HC, 978-1-893361-76-8 **$16.95**

Keeping Spiritual Balance as We Grow Older: More than 65 Creative Ways to Use Purpose, Prayer, and the Power of Spirit to Build a Meaningful Retirement
by Molly and Bernie Srode   8 x 8, 224 pp, Quality PB, 978-1-59473-042-9 **$16.99**

The Losses of Our Lives: The Sacred Gifts of Renewal in Everyday Loss
by Dr. Nancy Copeland-Payton   6 x 9, 192 pp, HC, 978-1-59473-271-3 **$19.99**

Money and the Way of Wisdom: Insights from the Book of Proverbs
by Timothy J. Sandoval, PhD   6 x 9, 192 pp, Quality PB, 978-1-59473-245-4 **$16.99**

Next to Godliness: Finding the Sacred in Housekeeping
Edited by Alice Peck   6 x 9, 224 pp, Quality PB, 978-1-59473-214-0 **$19.99**

Renewal in the Wilderness: A Spiritual Guide to Connecting with God in the Natural World   *by John Lionberger*
6 x 9, 176 pp, b/w photos, Quality PB, 978-1-59473-219-5 **$16.99**

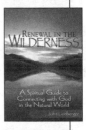

Sacred Attention: A Spiritual Practice for Finding God in the Moment
by Margaret D. McGee   6 x 9, 144 pp, Quality PB, 978-1-59473-291-1 **$16.99**

Soul Fire: Accessing Your Creativity
by Thomas Ryan, CSP   6 x 9, 160 pp, Quality PB, 978-1-59473-243-0 **$16.99**

A Spirituality for Brokenness: Discovering Your Deepest Self in Difficult Times
by Terry Taylor   6 x 9, 176 pp, Quality PB, 978-1-59473-229-4 **$16.99**

Spiritually Incorrect: Finding God in All the *Wrong* Places *by Dan Wakefield; Illus. by Marian DelVecchio*   5½ x 8½, 192 pp, b/w illus., Quality PB, 978-1-59473-137-2 **$15.99**

A Walk with Four Spiritual Guides: Krishna, Buddha, Jesus, and Ramakrishna
by Andrew Harvey   5½ x 8½, 192 pp, b/w photos & illus., Quality PB, 978-1-59473-138-9 **$15.99**

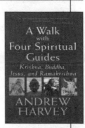

The Workplace and Spirituality: New Perspectives on Research and Practice
Edited by Dr. Joan Marques, Dr. Satinder Dhiman and Dr. Richard King
6 x 9, 256 pp, HC, 978-1-59473-260-7 **$29.99**

Spirituality & Crafts

Beading—The Creative Spirit: Finding Your Sacred Center through the Art of Beadwork *by Rev. Wendy Ellsworth*
Invites you on a spiritual pilgrimage into the kaleidoscope world of glass and color.   7 x 9, 240 pp, 8-page color insert, 40+ b/w photos and 40 diagrams, Quality PB, 978-1-59473-267-6 **$18.99**

Contemplative Crochet: A Hands-On Guide for Interlocking Faith and Craft *by Cindy Crandall-Frazier; Foreword by Linda Skolnik*
Illuminates the spiritual lessons you can learn through crocheting.
7 x 9, 208 pp, b/w photos, Quality PB, 978-1-59473-238-6 **$16.99**

The Knitting Way: A Guide to Spiritual Self-Discovery
by Linda Skolnik and Janice MacDaniels Examines how you can explore and strengthen your spiritual life through knitting.
7 x 9, 240 pp, b/w photos, Quality PB, 978-1-59473-079-5 **$16.99**

The Painting Path: Embodying Spiritual Discovery through Yoga, Brush and Color *by Linda Novick; Foreword by Richard Segalman*
Explores the divine connection you can experience through art.
7 x 9, 208 pp, 8-page color insert, plus b/w photos, Quality PB, 978-1-59473-226-3 **$18.99**

The Quilting Path: A Guide to Spiritual Discovery through Fabric, Thread and Kabbalah *by Louise Silk*
Explores how to cultivate personal growth through quilt making.
7 x 9, 192 pp, b/w photos and illus., Quality PB, 978-1-59473-206-5 **$16.99**

The Scrapbooking Journey: A Hands-On Guide to Spiritual Discovery
by Cory Richardson-Lauve; Foreword by Stacy Julian Reveals how this craft can become a practice used to deepen and shape your life.
7 x 9, 176 pp, 8-page color insert, plus b/w photos, Quality PB, 978-1-59473-216-4 **$18.99**

The Soulwork of Clay: A Hands-On Approach to Spirituality
by Marjory Zoet Bankson; Photos by Peter Bankson
Takes you through the seven-step process of making clay into a pot, drawing parallels at each stage to the process of spiritual growth.
7 x 9, 192 pp, b/w photos, Quality PB, 978-1-59473-249-2 **$16.99**

Kabbalah / Enneagram
(Books from Jewish Lights Publishing, SkyLight Paths' sister imprint)

Cast in God's Image: Discover Your Personality Type Using the Enneagram and Kabbalah
by Rabbi Howard A. Addison 7 x 9, 176 pp, Quality PB, 978-1-58023-124-4 **$16.95**

Ehyeh: A Kabbalah for Tomorrow *by Dr. Arthur Green*
6 x 9, 224 pp, Quality PB, 978-1-58023-213-5 **$16.99**

The Enneagram and Kabbalah, 2nd Edition: Reading Your Soul
by Rabbi Howard A. Addison 6 x 9, 192 pp, Quality PB, 978-1-58023-229-6 **$16.99**

The Gift of Kabbalah: Discovering the Secrets of Heaven, Renewing Your Life on Earth
by Tamar Frankiel, PhD 6 x 9, 256 pp, Quality PB, 978-1-58023-141-1 **$16.95**

God in Your Body: Kabbalah, Mindfulness and Embodied Spiritual Practice
by Jay Michaelson 6 x 9, 272 pp, Quality PB, 978-1-58023-304-0 **$18.99**

Kabbalah: A Brief Introduction for Christians
by Tamar Frankiel, PhD 5½ x 8½, 208 pp, Quality PB, 978-1-58023-303-3 **$16.99**

Zohar: Annotated & Explained *Translation & Annotation by Daniel C. Matt; Foreword by Andrew Harvey* 5½ x 8½, 176 pp, Quality PB, 978-1-893361-51-5 **$15.99**

Spiritual Practice

Laugh Your Way to Grace: Reclaiming the Spiritual Power of Humor
by Rev. Susan Sparks   A powerful, humorous case for laughter as a spiritual, healing path.   6 x 9, 176 pp, Quality PB, 978-1-59473-280-5 **$16.99**

Haiku—The Sacred Art: A Spiritual Practice in Three Lines
by Margaret D. McGee   Introduces haiku as a simple and effective way of tapping into the sacred moments that permeate everyday living.
5½ x 8½, 192 pp, Quality PB, 978-1-59473-269-0 **$16.99**

Dance—The Sacred Art: The Joy of Movement as a Spiritual Practice
by Cynthia Winton-Henry   Invites all of us, regardless of experience, into the possibility of dance/movement as a spiritual practice.
5½ x 8½, 224 pp, Quality PB, 978-1-59473-268-3 **$16.99**

Spiritual Adventures in the Snow: Skiing & Snowboarding as Renewal for Your Soul   by Dr. Marcia McFee and Rev. Karen Foster; Foreword by Paul Arthur
Explores snow sports as tangible experiences of the spiritual essence of our bodies and the earth.   5½ x 8½, 208 pp, Quality PB, 978-1-59473-270-6 **$16.99**

Divining the Body: Reclaim the Holiness of Your Physical Self   by Jan Phillips
8 x 8, 256 pp, Quality PB, 978-1-59473-080-1 **$16.99**

Everyday Herbs in Spiritual Life: A Guide to Many Practices
by Michael J. Caduto; Foreword by Rosemary Gladstar
7 x 9, 208 pp, 20+ b/w illus., Quality PB, 978-1-59473-174-7 **$16.99**

The Gospel of Thomas: A Guidebook for Spiritual Practice
by Ron Miller; Translations by Stevan Davies   6 x 9, 160 pp, Quality PB, 978-1-59473-047-4 **$14.99**

Hospitality—The Sacred Art: Discovering the Hidden Spiritual Power of Invitation and Welcome   by Rev. Nanette Sawyer; Foreword by Rev. Dirk Ficca
5½ x 8½, 208 pp, Quality PB, 978-1-59473-228-7 **$16.99**

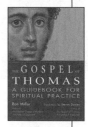

Labyrinths from the Outside In: Walking to Spiritual Insight—A Beginner's Guide   by Donna Schaper and Carole Ann Camp
6 x 9, 208 pp, b/w illus. and photos, Quality PB, 978-1-893361-18-8 **$16.95**

Practicing the Sacred Art of Listening: A Guide to Enrich Your Relationships and Kindle Your Spiritual Life   by Kay Lindahl   8 x 8, 176 pp, Quality PB, 978-1-893361-85-0 **$16.95**

Recovery—The Sacred Art: The Twelve Steps as Spiritual Practice   by Rami Shapiro; Foreword by Joan Borysenko, PhD   5½ x 8½, 240 pp, Quality PB, 978-1-59473-259-1 **$16.99**

Running—The Sacred Art: Preparing to Practice   by Dr. Warren A. Kay; Foreword by Kristin Armstrong   5½ x 8½, 160 pp, Quality PB, 978-1-59473-227-0 **$16.99**

The Sacred Art of Bowing: Preparing to Practice
by Andi Young   5½ x 8½, 128 pp, b/w illus., Quality PB, 978-1-893361-82-9 **$14.95**

The Sacred Art of Chant: Preparing to Practice
by Ana Hernández   5½ x 8½, 192 pp, Quality PB, 978-1-59473-036-8 **$15.99**

The Sacred Art of Fasting: Preparing to Practice
by Thomas Ryan, CSP   5½ x 8½, 192 pp, Quality PB, 978-1-59473-078-8 **$15.99**

The Sacred Art of Forgiveness: Forgiving Ourselves and Others through God's Grace
by Marcia Ford   8 x 8, 176 pp, Quality PB, 978-1-59473-175-4 **$16.99**

The Sacred Art of Listening: Forty Reflections for Cultivating a Spiritual Practice
by Kay Lindahl; Illus. by Amy Schnapper   8 x 8, 160 pp, b/w illus., Quality PB, 978-1-893361-44-7 **$16.99**

The Sacred Art of Lovingkindness: Preparing to Practice
by Rabbi Rami Shapiro; Foreword by Marcia Ford   5½ x 8½, 176 pp, Quality PB, 978-1-59473-151-8 **$16.99**

Sacred Attention: A Spiritual Practice for Finding God in the Moment
by Margaret D. McGee   6 x 9, 144 pp, Quality PB, 978-1-59473-291-1 **$16.99**

Sacred Speech: A Practical Guide for Keeping Spirit in Your Speech
by Rev. Donna Schaper   6 x 9, 176 pp, Quality PB, 978-1-59473-068-9 **$15.99**
HC, 978-1-893361-74-4 **$21.95**

Soul Fire: Accessing Your Creativity
by Thomas Ryan, CSP   6 x 9, 160 pp, Quality PB, 978-1-59473-243-0 **$16.99**

Thanking & Blessing—The Sacred Art: Spiritual Vitality through Gratefulness
by Jay Marshall, PhD; Foreword by Philip Gulley   5½ x 8½, 176 pp, Quality PB, 978-1-59473-231-7 **$16.99**

Prayer / Meditation

Sacred Attention: A Spiritual Practice for Finding God in the Moment
by Margaret D. McGee
Framed on the Christian liturgical year, this inspiring guide explores ways to develop a practice of attention as a means of talking—and listening—to God.
6 x 9, 144 pp, Quality PB, 978-1-59473-291-1 **$16.99**

Women Pray: Voices through the Ages, from Many Faiths, Cultures and Traditions
Edited and with Introductions by Monica Furlong
5 x 7¼, 256 pp, Quality PB, 978-1-59473-071-9 **$15.99**

Women of Color Pray: Voices of Strength, Faith, Healing, Hope and Courage
Edited and with Introductions by Christal M. Jackson
Through these prayers, poetry, lyrics, meditations and affirmations, you will share in the strong and undeniable connection women of color share with God.
5 x 7¼, 208 pp, Quality PB, 978-1-59473-077-1 **$15.99**

Secrets of Prayer: A Multifaith Guide to Creating Personal Prayer in Your Life   *by Nancy Corcoran, CSJ*
This compelling, multifaith guidebook offers you companionship and encouragement on the journey to a healthy prayer life. 6 x 9, 160 pp, Quality PB, 978-1-59473-215-7 **$16.99**

Prayers to an Evolutionary God
by William Cleary; Afterword by Diarmuid O'Murchu
Inspired by the spiritual and scientific teachings of Diarmuid O'Murchu and Teilhard de Chardin, reveals that religion and science can be combined to create an expanding view of the universe—an evolutionary faith.
6 x 9, 208 pp, HC, 978-1-59473-006-1 **$21.99**

The Art of Public Prayer, 2nd Edition: Not for Clergy Only
by Lawrence A. Hoffman, PhD 6 x 9, 288 pp, Quality PB, 978-1-893361-06-5 **$19.99**

A Heart of Stillness: A Complete Guide to Learning the Art of Meditation
by David A. Cooper 5½ x 8½, 272 pp, Quality PB, 978-1-893361-03-4 **$18.99**

Meditation without Gurus: A Guide to the Heart of Practice
by Clark Strand 5½ x 8½, 192 pp, Quality PB, 978-1-893361-93-5 **$16.95**

Praying with Our Hands: 21 Practices of Embodied Prayer from the World's Spiritual Traditions   *by Jon M. Sweeney; Photos by Jennifer J. Wilson; Foreword by Mother Tessa Bielecki; Afterword by Taitetsu Unno, PhD*
8 x 8, 96 pp, 22 duotone photos, Quality PB, 978-1-893361-16-4 **$16.95**

Three Gates to Meditation Practice: A Personal Journey into Sufism, Buddhism, and Judaism   *by David A. Cooper* 5½ x 8½, 240 pp, Quality PB, 978-1-893361-22-5 **$16.95**

Prayer / M. Basil Pennington, OCSO

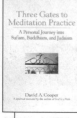

Finding Grace at the Center, 3rd Edition: The Beginning of Centering Prayer   *with Thomas Keating, OCSO, and Thomas E. Clarke, SJ; Foreword by Rev. Cynthia Bourgeault, PhD* A practical guide to a simple and beautiful form of meditative prayer. 5 x 7¼, 128 pp, Quality PB, 978-1-59473-182-2 **$12.99**

The Monks of Mount Athos: A Western Monk's Extraordinary Spiritual Journey on Eastern Holy Ground   *Foreword by Archimandrite Dionysios*
Explores the landscape, monastic communities and food of Athos.
6 x 9, 352 pp, Quality PB, 978-1-893361-78-2 **$18.95**

Psalms: A Spiritual Commentary   *Illus. by Phillip Ratner*
Reflections on some of the most beloved passages from the Bible's most widely read book.   6 x 9, 176 pp, 24 full-page b/w illus., Quality PB, 978-1-59473-234-8 **$16.99**

The Song of Songs: A Spiritual Commentary   *Illus. by Phillip Ratner*
Explore the Bible's most challenging mystical text.
6 x 9, 160 pp, 14 full-page b/w illus., Quality PB, 978-1-59473-235-5 **$16.99**
HC, 978-1-59473-004-7 **$19.99**

Women's Interest

New Feminist Christianity: Many Voices, Many Views
Edited by Mary E. Hunt and Diann L. Neu
Insights from ministers and theologians, activists and leaders, artists and liturgists who are shaping the future. Taken together, their voices offer a starting point for building new models of religious life and worship.
6 x 9, 384 pp, HC, 978-1-59473-285-0 **$24.99**

New Jewish Feminism: Probing the Past, Forging the Future
Edited by Rabbi Elyse Goldstein; Foreword by Anita Diamant
Looks at the growth and accomplishments of Jewish feminism and what they mean for Jewish women today and tomorrow. Features the voices of women from every area of Jewish life, addressing the important issues that concern Jewish women.
6 x 9, 480 pp, HC, 978-1-58023-359-0 **$24.99***

Dance—The Sacred Art: The Joy of Movement as a Spiritual Practice
by Cynthia Winton-Henry 5½ x 8½, 224 pp, Quality PB, 978-1-59473-268-3 **$16.99**

Daughters of the Desert: Stories of Remarkable Women from Christian, Jewish and Muslim Traditions
by Claire Rudolf Murphy, Meghan Nuttall Sayres, Mary Cronk Farrell, Sarah Conover and Betsy Wharton
5½ x 8½, 192 pp, Illus., Quality PB, 978-1-59473-106-8 **$14.99** Inc. reader's discussion guide
HC, 978-1-893361-72-0 **$19.95**

The Divine Feminine in Biblical Wisdom Literature
Selections Annotated & Explained
Translation & Annotation by Rabbi Rami Shapiro; Foreword by Rev. Cynthia Bourgeault, PhD
5½ x 8½, 240 pp, Quality PB, 978-1-59473-109-9 **$16.99**

Divining the Body: Reclaim the Holiness of Your Physical Self
by Jan Phillips 8 x 8, 256 pp, Quality PB, 978-1-59473-080-1 **$16.99**

Honoring Motherhood: Prayers, Ceremonies & Blessings
Edited and with Introductions by Lynn L. Caruso 5 x 7¼, 272 pp, HC, 978-1-59473-239-3 **$19.99**

ReVisions: Seeing Torah through a Feminist Lens
by Rabbi Elyse Goldstein 5½ x 8½, 224 pp, Quality PB, 978-1-58023-117-6 **$16.95***

The Triumph of Eve & Other Subversive Bible Tales
by Matt Biers-Ariel 5½ x 8½, 192 pp, Quality PB, 978-1-59473-176-1 **$14.99**
Also available: **The Triumph of Eve Teacher's Guide**
8½ x 11, 44 pp, PB, 978-1-59473-152-5 **$8.99**

White Fire: A Portrait of Women Spiritual Leaders in America
by Malka Drucker; Photos by Gay Block 7 x 10, 320 pp, b/w photos, HC, 978-1-893361-64-5 **$24.95**

Woman Spirit Awakening in Nature
Growing Into the Fullness of Who You Are
by Nancy Barrett Chickerneo, PhD; Foreword by Eileen Fisher
8 x 8, 224 pp, b/w illus., Quality PB, 978-1-59473-250-8 **$16.99**

Women of Color Pray: Voices of Strength, Faith, Healing, Hope and Courage
Edited and with Introductions by Christal M. Jackson
5 x 7¼, 208 pp, Quality PB, 978-1-59473-077-1 **$15.99**

Women Pray: Voices through the Ages, from Many Faiths, Cultures and Traditions
Edited and with Introductions by Monica Furlong
5 x 7¼, 256 pp, Quality PB, 978-1-59473-071-9 **$15.99**

The Women's Haftarah Commentary: New Insights from Women Rabbis on the 54 Weekly Haftarah Portions, the 5 Megillot & Special Shabbatot *Edited by Rabbi Elyse Goldstein*
6 x 9, 560 pp, Quality PB, 978-1-58023-371-2 **$19.99***

The Women's Torah Commentary: New Insights from Women Rabbis on the 54 Weekly Torah Portions *Edited by Rabbi Elyse Goldstein*
6 x 9, 496 pp, Quality PB, 978-1-58023-370-5 **$19.99**; HC, 978-1-58023-076-6 **$34.95***

* A book from Jewish Lights, SkyLight Paths' sister imprint

About SKYLIGHT PATHS Publishing

SkyLight Paths Publishing is creating a place where people of different spiritual traditions come together for challenge and inspiration, a place where we can help each other understand the mystery that lies at the heart of our existence.

Through spirituality, our religious beliefs are increasingly becoming a part of our lives—rather than *apart* from our lives. While many of us may be more interested than ever in spiritual growth, we may be less firmly planted in traditional religion. Yet, we do want to deepen our relationship to the sacred, to learn from our own as well as from other faith traditions, and to practice in new ways.

SkyLight Paths sees both believers and seekers as a community that increasingly transcends traditional boundaries of religion and denomination—people wanting to learn from each other, *walking together, finding the way.*

For your information and convenience, at the back of this book we have provided a list of other SkyLight Paths books you might find interesting and useful. They cover the following subjects:

Buddhism / Zen	Global Spiritual	Monasticism
Catholicism	Perspectives	Mysticism
Children's Books	Gnosticism	Poetry
Christianity	Hinduism /	Prayer
Comparative	Vedanta	Religious Etiquette
Religion	Inspiration	Retirement
Current Events	Islam / Sufism	Spiritual Biography
Earth-Based	Judaism	Spiritual Direction
Spirituality	Kabbalah	Spirituality
Enneagram	Meditation	Women's Interest
	Midrash Fiction	Worship

Or phone, fax, mail or e-mail to: SKYLIGHT PATHS Publishing
Sunset Farm Offices, Route 4 • P.O. Box 237 • Woodstock, Vermont 05091
Tel: (802) 457-4000 • Fax: (802) 457-4004 • www.skylightpaths.com
Credit card orders: (800) 962-4544 (8:30AM–5:30PM ET Monday–Friday)
Generous discounts on quantity orders. SATISFACTION GUARANTEED. Prices subject to change.

X